HAUNTED

ISLE OF

SHEPPEY

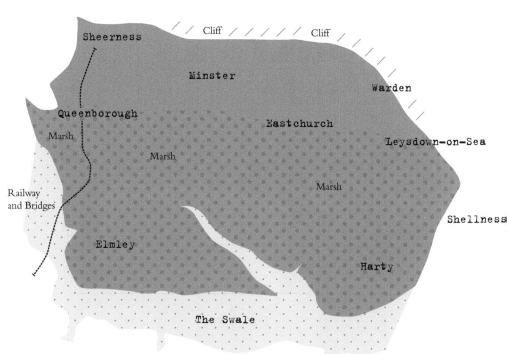

Thames Estuary

Cliff / / / / / / Cliff /

Sheerness

Minster

Warden

Queenborough

Eastchurch

Marsh

Marsh

Leysdown-on-Sea

Marsh

Railway
and Bridges

Shellness

Elmley

Harty

The Swale

Kent Mainland

HAUNTED
ISLE OF
SHEPPEY

Neil Arnold

The
History
Press

This book is dedicated to
Jacqui, Charlie & Morgan

First published 2014
Reprinted 2020

The History Press
97 St George's Place, Cheltenham
Gloucestershire, GL50 3QB
www.thehistorypress.co.uk

British Library Cataloguing in Publication Data.
A catalogue record for this book is available from the British Library.

ISBN 978 0 7509 5213 2

Typesetting and origination by The History Press
Printed in Great Britain by TJ International Ltd, Padstow, Cornwall.

CONTENTS

ACKNOWLEDGEMENTS

'This is Sheppey ... the Isle of Sheppey – the island jewel of Kent.'

Charles Igglesden

Many thanks to the following – my wife Jemma, my mum (Paulene) and dad (Ron), my sister Vicki, and my grandparents Ron and Win. Thanks also to Emma Grove at the *Sheerness Times Guardian* and The History Press. I am grateful to the *East Kent Gazette*, *Sheppey Gazette*, Medway Archives & Local Studies, Sheerness Library, Elaine Price, David Sage, Trevor Edwards, Paul Langridge, Gary Dobner, Steve and Janet, Blue Town Heritage Centre, Simon Wyatt, Roger Betts, Alice Bodiam, Elsie and Brian, Bob Frost, Betty Oldmeadow, Paul Deadman, Philip Charles, Brian Slade, Mai Griffin, Lee Waters, Cassandra Eason, Paul Dummott, Paula Bailey, Tony Stubley, Sheila M. Judge (1920–2002), Colin Penney, Sheppey Matters, Lena Crowder and Minster Abbey Gatehouse Museum, *Kent News*, Kent Online, Sheppey Website, Charles Igglesden, Kent History Forum, and The Sheppey History Page.

All photographs are by the author unless stated otherwise.

FOREWORD

With haunted houses, ghostly ghouls and mythical monsters, Sheppey has its fair share of spooky stories. The tales are the types that keep tongues wagging and our readers at the *Sheerness Times Guardian* never tire of hearing them so it's great to have people like Neil Arnold keeping these legends alive.

Neil was one of the first people I came into contact with when I started reporting on the paper and he's featured regularly in my stories over the years, mainly about sightings of Sheppey's mystery big cat. This is the one which intrigues me most, both as a reporter and a resident. So many islanders claim to have seen it; when they give me their stories and their descriptions, they are so clear, and witnesses are always adamant about what they've seen. Many of them were previously sceptics, but now they've seen it there is no doubt in their minds. I can't decide 100 per cent whether I think it's actually out there or whether there's a less exciting explanation for it, but I love the idea that it does exist and I never get bored of listening to people's stories. I lean more towards thinking there must be something in it – too

many people have sightings of it for it to be nothing. The most frustrating thing is the lack of solid evidence, especially in this age of mobile phones, so I'm holding out for the day when we get that all important photo and, of course, when I finally catch a glimpse myself. Although having said that, Neil's research has lead him to discover paw prints and animal carcasses, so it's a great debate.

But it's not just the cat: *Haunted Isle of Sheppey* is full of other classic tales too, including the ghostly maid who is said to reside at Shurland Hall and the Grey Lady of Minster Abbey, who has been seen in the church grounds.

By their very nature, these ones are harder to capture on film and therefore perhaps harder to believe. I would definitely have to see something pretty definitive for me to believe in the supernatural and life beyond the grave, but whatever your view, the book makes for interesting reading.

Emma Grove, 2014

Emma Grove is a senior reporter at the *Sheerness Times Guardian* and has worked there since 2008. She lives on the island.

INTRODUCTION

'The longer you linger in this famous little island, the deeper the fascination grows.'

Charles Igglesden

'Ghosts! Well, there are such things, so why not write about them?'

Mrs Stella Stocker

There are two visits to the Isle of Sheppey – situated off the north coast of Kent – which I'll never forget. The first was when I was a child, it was a warm summer's day in the late 1970s or early '80s and I was accompanied by my parents and grandparents. I remember looking out to sea from Leysdown and exclaiming that the glistening water was 'like a big bath', so in awe was I by the stretch of grey-blue of the North Sea, the likes of which I'd never seen before. Then, just a few years ago I visited the island with my father – it was a freezing cold, snow-laden day and we were on the track of a melanistic leopard (a black panther) long rumoured to have prowled the marshes. I doubt very much on that particularly bitter day that even an elusive big cat would have been

The Isle of Sheppey – marshland as far as the eye can see.

tempted to rear its feline head, such was the climate. The island was pristine white and the stark trees lining the country lanes seemed to be reaching into the pallid sky, but stranger still, the birds perched on the branches had literally frozen to death and hung upside down like macabre Christmas decorations. The morbid spectacle was something akin to a creaky horror film. I recall attempting to film the scenery – my hands could not stand the cold – but, despite not filming the shy exotic cat, the rumours still persist to this day. Many scoff at the legend of the local 'big cat', and there are even those who claim that such an animal is a ghostly manifestation of some long-deceased circus escapee. However, an island resident named Paul Deadman confirmed that unusual 'pets' had often been kept on Sheppey; he once told me:

> There definitely used to be a lion living at Leysdown, it was in a cage above another building. I'm sure it was at a place called the Island Country Club and Hotel which is now a care home. I used to live at Warden Bay as a kid and we used to walk past it all the time to have a look! Also the Cross Brothers' circus originally came from the island as well; they used to have the yard that is now a tyre firm at Blue Town. There used to be monkeys, a lion and various other cats all crammed into small cages! This was in the early/mid 1980s. I well remember sitting in the Cosy Cafe in Leysdown in around '85 and the owner walked up the street with a tiger cub on a lead! I also remember the puma along the lower road; the man that had it was my dad's mates nephew and he apparently had two when they were small but became too much as they got older!

The Isle of Sheppey is an atmospheric place indeed, and, by the sounds of it, the ideal place for a surreal safari! However, despite only covering some 36 sq.miles (older records state 21 sq. miles, excluding the once smaller islets situated off the coast such as the islands of Elmley and Harty which eventually became part of the main island before the channels separating them literally filled up with silt), it is an environment steeped in history and some of it is rather ghastly. For instance, the isle is certainly one that freely gives up its dead – at Minster Abbey a 1,300-year-old head belonging to an Anglo-Saxon nun was unearthed during an excavation. In the 1920s more than twenty skeletons were unearthed in Minster and elsewhere skeletal remains of infants dating back roughly 500 years were found. In volume 28 of *A Saunter Through Kent With Pen and Pencil*, chronicler Charles Igglesden writes of Sheppey as consisting of 'marshy pastures dotted with strange mounds, lanes overshadowed by elms and winding among the hills, old world churches and rustic homesteads and always glimpses of the sea to the north'. The 'strange mounds' of which he speaks were once believed to have been burial places of the Danes (said to have ravaged the island on several occasions beginning in the ninth century) or other warriors, slain when the Dutch invaded in the seventeenth century. Although the Dutch only stayed on the island for eleven days, much bloodshed was caused, with Igglesden remarking that 'Here the soil was more deeply blood-stained than any other part of England during the invasion ...'

A more prosaic explanation for those mounds, however, is that they were constructed and used by shepherds many years ago in order to save sheep from drowning due to terrible floods which swept the island. Again Igglesden writes: 'Here came the floods that swept the levels and drowned the long-haired sheep of Sheppey by the thousand, and shepherds too,' but he was quick to dismiss the legends pertaining to the mounds as burial plots, stating, 'I'm sorry to explode the old legend but no excavations have disclosed the skeletons of dead Saxon warriors or Viking kings'.

Another rumour to abound from the island focuses on flora, for it was once recorded by a Donald Maxwell in his book *The Seven Islands of Kent* that, 'there is to be found growing in the marshes of the Swale, and said [on what authority I do not know] to grow nowhere else, a low growing plant with a dull red bloom known as Dane's Blood'. The flower, in folklore anyway, seems to be a symbol of the massacre of the Danes.

The name Sheppey is said to derive from the Saxon word *sceapige* – meaning the island of sheep. It is said that the first ever lamb bred in England was at Sheppey, although this may have been imported Roman stock, because as Mr Igglesden states, '… we do not find them [sheep] in Caesar's list of animals, which he found in this country and indigenous to it'.

It was the Romans who considered the stretch of the Swale – which separates Sheppey (at that time known as Insula Ovium) from the mainland – to be of great importance for their travels. Their ships would no doubt have travelled from the River Wantsum off east Kent to the area of Sheppey known now as Shellness. Even so, despite the varying invasions, numerous settlers and

eroding cliffs, the island has stood the test of time. However, ancient history has very much embedded itself into the Sheppey coastline. Every now and then numerous fossils dating back millions of years are unearthed, especially around the beaches of Sheerness. Giant turtles, crocodiles, elephants, snakes, huge birds and all manner of plant life as well as ancient serpents have been found over the last handful of centuries entombed within the rocks and clay. Nowadays of course, the island is inhabited by almost 40,000 people, but most of these reside in built-up pockets on the island, leaving the rest of the land to soggy marsh and sprawling fields.

It's no real surprise that wildlife is rife on Sheppey, although it was rumoured in the early 1900s that no fox, mole or rat inhabited the island. This is contradicted, however, by the belief that the church at Elmley was so rarely visited due to a sinister plague of rats which would drive visitors away. The former village was once described as 'one of the loneliest spots in Kent' and was once believed to have been a setting for human sacrifice!

Coming back to the island's wildlife, in the 1860s a colony of European yellow-tailed scorpions were discovered living at the Sheerness docks, in healthy numbers. They are believed to have been imported on a ship, as they are usually native to southern Europe and north-west Africa. In 1997 the presumed-extinct Maid of Kent beetle turned up in a lavatory on the island. The 1in long insect, which resembles a golden-haired bee, was apparently last seen in Kent in 1950 and reported officially endangered during the 1980s. It was also recorded that in the June of 1756 a huge whale, measuring approximately

36ft in length and weighing 'many tons' was caught at Minster-on-Sea. Another whale, of the humpback variety and measuring almost 40ft in length, was found dead off Sheppey in the spring of 2013. In 1972 a dolphin was found washed ashore at Leysdown, while in '64 a plague of poisonous jellyfish invaded the Sheppey coastline. In 2012 an even stranger out-of-place animal turned up on the island – albeit dead. A wallaby (a marsupial native to Australia) had somehow made its way across from the mainland. Press at the time believed that the animal had swum across the Swale; either that or it had obtained a cheap day return on the train. The animal was more likely an escapee from a private collection and sadly, it was eventually hit by a car. Mind you, in the autumn of 1912, the island was said to have been briefly visited by even weirder invaders – aliens! On 14 October 1912 what became known as the 'Sheerness scare' hit the headlines after numerous island residents reported a strange buzzing noise emanating from the night sky. No craft was actually seen, despite numerous lookouts being stationed across the island. Many feared that a German Zeppelin airship was to blame and the scare was addressed in the House of Commons during late November with Prime Minister Winston Churchill commenting that some 'thing' had most certainly been experienced. However, with no British aircraft in the skies at the time and the nearest foreign Zeppelin being some 400 miles away, no one was quite sure what had spooked so many people. Weirder still, at 10.30 p.m. on the night of 22 March 1979, local police received several phone calls from motorists who claimed to have seen a bizarre entity near the Kingsferry Bridge

at Sheppey Way. Witnesses described a 'creature' dressed in a silvery costume akin to a diving suit, but resembling an ape in form – maybe that unidentified flying object of 1912 had dropped some 'thing' off! Despite investigations, police could find no trace of the humanoid; some of the reports seemed to contradict one another, with one male motorist claiming that the face of the being could not be seen because it wore a helmet with a black visor. Consider also that a majority of the vehicles travelling over the bridge were clocking an average speed of 30–40mph; one wonders if they'd merely seen somebody walking late at night. We'll never know if there really was a Sheppey 'space ape' or simply a person in rather unusual fancy dress. Whatever this character was, one male witness – a lorry driver – was so spooked by its appearance that when he got home that night he took a shotgun to bed with him whilst another claimed that the being was a ghost!

The so-called Sheppey 'space ape' enigma may not have been solved, but several years previously, in 1967, one reputed Sheppey alien invasion was. The armed forces, members of the Ministry of Defence and several police officers were called into action when a handful of strange disc-like objects turned up across the south-east. One such 'flying saucer' was discovered at Sheppey. At the time a number of people had truly begun to believe that the island was being invaded by Martians until bomb disposal experts, X-raying the disc, discovered a set of batteries. The disc simply turned out to be part of a huge hoax carried out by a bunch of university students who had planned the 'saucer' flap as part of their rag week.

They'd placed six discs – which resembled sci-fi-style alien spacecraft – seemingly in strategic fashion across southern England, and even filled some of the discs with a peculiar gooey substance to give the effect of extraterrestrial content!

Nowadays access to the island doesn't have to come via flying saucer! Two main bridges cross the Swale, the most recent of these – the Sheppey Crossing – being constructed in May 2006 to ease the flow of traffic that would often find itself lined up on the Kingsferry Bridge, a lifting bridge built in 1959 to allow ships to pass beneath it. There have been a handful of bridges built over the years connecting Sheppey to the mainland. Charles Igglesden believes there may have been some type of structure in place as early as the fourteenth century which connected Sheppey to Elmley, although

it was destroyed by a large wave. Before the first main bridge in the 1860s, it was believed that people were transported across the river by a small ferry. However, the trip would have been made a lot easier in 1779 when the Thames froze and a sheet of ice stretched from the island to Essex!

Ever since childhood I've been interested in the quirky and eerie side of history, particularly of local antiquity; those macabre tales and ghostly yarns which often leave readers scratching their head in bemusement. Sheppey has one of Britain's most famous legends pertaining to a chap named Sir Robert de Shurland. His tragic tale is one that has become urban legend, passed down through generations, at times altered to fit in with the current climate. The yarn refers to an interesting tomb situated in

View from Sheppey Way of the Sheppey Crossing – a bridge built in 2006 to allow further access to the island.

The tomb of Sir Robert de Shurland at Minster Abbey. Note the horse's head at his feet.

Minster Abbey church. The vault depicts a resting knight accompanied by a horse's head which appears to be rising out of waves by his feet. Many believe the horse is called Grey Dolphin and that it was mounted by de Shurland in the late thirteenth and early fourteenth centuries. Sir Robert, due to his gallantry in battle, was given the right by Edward I to comb the shores of Sheppey with his lance and take home whatever flotsam and jetsam he should find. However, de Shurland became involved in an unfortunate incident which many believed would lead to his eventual death.

Whilst some say the story is a fable, possibly originating from the seventeenth century and elaborated on over the succeeding years, it is still one of intrigue, for it is said that de Shurland once killed a monk who failed to respond to his orders. Sir Robert became ridden with guilt after committing this act and so decided to visit the king in order to be pardoned. At the time the king was said to have been in a boat moored off Sheerness.

Sir Robert, on Grey Dolphin, rode along the beach with haste and then dismounted before swimming to the king's location. Although the king forgave Sir Robert, once back on shore the knight was approached by a witch who told him matter-of-factly that Grey Dolphin, which had saved his life by transporting him at pace to the king, would eventually be the death of him. Legend has it that de Shurland was so disturbed by the woman's prediction that he dismounted from his horse and with his sword beheaded the poor animal there and then.

A few years later, whilst walking along the same stretch of beach, Sir Robert was once again confronted by the cackling hag who mocked him. In a fit of rage, the knight kicked the ground but received a nasty cut from a sharp object. The splinter turned out to be a shard of bone from the buried skull of Grey Dolphin and a few days later the wound became infected and Sir Robert de Shurland eventually died of blood poisoning.

Despite its strange and bloody history, my favourite legends about the island concern its reputed ghosts and ghouls. Just like a modern-day Charles Igglesden, I've not only scoured the archives but also the hedgerows and marshes in reference to this ancient isle in search of creepy and curious tales of things that go bump not just in the night, but the daytime too. Surprisingly, ghost stories attached to the island are not that easy to come by, but that's not so unusual when one looks at the vast marshlands which sprawl across the landmass.

Ghosts are likely to intrigue the minds of mankind for thousands of years to come, but it's unlikely we'll ever prove their existence. However, I feel it is my aim to chronicle many of these local tales – some known, some unknown – and collate them so that when I too have passed over to the other side, historians, ghost hunters, and members of the public alike can flick through them by the light of a flickering candle. Do remember, however, that many of the places where these spirits are said to haunt are private property, and that some of the stories must be taken with a pinch of salt, as some are certainly vaguer than others. With ghosts it's simply about the mystery and the fun of investigating them – although I'm pretty sure that should you see one, especially if you are of a sceptical nature, it becomes a whole new ballgame. For now, however, I present to you *Haunted Isle of Sheppey*; a collection of some of my favourite local tales. I'm sorry I could not fit every spook tale from the island in. But let us not dither; and so with haste grab your coat, scarf, gloves and trusty torch and let us head forth across the marshes, into the night.

Neil Arnold, 2014

The Author

Neil Arnold is a full-time monster hunter, folklorist and author of many books including *Haunted Maidstone*, *Haunted Ashford*, *Haunted Chatham*, *Haunted Rochester*, *Haunted Bromley*, *Haunted Tunbridge Wells*, *Paranormal Kent*, *Shadows in the Sky: The Haunted Airways of Britain*, *Shadows on the Sea: The Maritime Mysteries of Britain*, *Monster! – The A-Z of Zooform Phenomena*, and *Mystery Animals of the British Isles: Kent*. He runs regular ghost walks around Rochester and Blue Bell Hill.

'There are, it is true, few places so interesting as Sheppey, but why, apart from its history? Just because its scenery is so weird, its surroundings so outlandish.'

C.G. Harper

1

SHIVERS AT SHEERNESS

Situated close to the mouth of the River Medway, the town of Sheerness, known for its docks, can be found on the north-west corner of the island. Henry VIII ordered the construction of a fort at Sheerness to prevent enemy ships entering the River Medway to lay siege upon Chatham Dockyard. One of the strangest, non-ghost-related stories to come from the town emerged from the late 1950s when a local resident was attacked by a honey bear whilst he slept. The animal, which the man had been keeping as a pet, had been locked in the bathroom but was released by accident by his wife. The victim of the attack suffered deep scratches to his head, face and hands and told the local press that the incident was 'bizarre in the extreme'. The honey bear was taken in by London Zoo.

This Old House etc.

The Old House at Home is not the name of some creaking Gothic mansion, but the title of a public house situated in Sheerness High Street. The pub dates back to the seventeenth century and it is said to be haunted by an unseen presence that likes to move items of furniture. The pub website speaks of 'inexplicable noises on the stairs', but every time such a clamour is reported and then investigated, no one can actually be found within the vicinity to explain the racket. A couple of years ago an investigative team visited the Castle Tavern in Sheerness to conduct paranormal research. The team were following up a report made by a barmaid who claimed that upon entering the gloomy basement she'd been hit on the back of the head by a barrel top, even though no one else was in the area. On a creepier note it has been claimed by owners that on certain nights whilst sleeping they are attacked, and at times thrown out of bed. Such a terrifying experience nods to fictional horror films such as *Paranormal Activity*, but the reality is far more frightening. In numerous buildings across the island, ranging from pubs to houses, staff and residents have reported waking up of a

The Old House at Home public house in Sheerness.

night unable to move, at times sensing a presence in the room and then a crushing weight upon their chest. This is often known as sleep paralysis, but cannot simply be explained by someone being stressed, overly tired, or having eaten too much cheese, as in some cases witnesses have described seeing a shadowy figure or something akin to an old, decrepit hag-like woman in the room.

Sadly, those who've investigated the pub have only photographed what researchers tend to call orbs – which are apparently peculiar anomalies that seem to appear in a majority of photographs, especially when taken by digital cameras. Are such orbs ghostly manifestations or mere light, moisture or dust anomalies and camera glitches? In 2007 a Sheppey resident who had set up a security camera alongside his home got a surprise

the following day when he watched the footage the CCTV had captured: he saw a weird, white orb-light object drift in front of the house and down the side alley. Those who viewed the film argued that the weird sphere may have been an insect or dust particle but such anomalies could well explain old reports of what are termed as will-o'-the-wisps or even UFOs (unidentified flying objects).

Blue Town, which can be found at Sheerness, has its origins in the small hulks situated in the estuary in which the dockyard workers used to reside. The workers then went on to build small cabins which were painted a blue-grey colour (according to legend the paint used had been stolen) and over time this area became a small community centred upon such blue dwellings. Sadly, according to the Sheppey Website, these

Blue Town – the haunt of a ghost or two.

living conditions were even worse than the original hulks, with many of the workers dying from malaria due to the swarms of mosquitos which came off the marshes (although in 2002 a scientist dismissed such rumours). Those who perished were buried in a small island off Queenborough which became known as Deadman's Island, with the website confirming that, 'it's still checked regularly to make sure the diseases are gradually dying away'.

Intriguingly Deadman's Island has one of Kent's most bizarre ghost stories attached to it. In 1950 two intrepid journalists, Frederick Sanders and Duncan Rand, took the brave step in exploring Deadman's Island. To them, tales of the remote area were rife with rumour that, two centuries previously, Napoleonic soldiers taken prisoner by the British were buried at the spot, many having died as a result of plague. However, when Sanders and his colleague were ferried to the mist-enshrouded location, they believed that something monstrous had been present. Several coffins lay strewn about the place and the skeletons which were exposed were bereft of skulls, leading the explorers to believe in the existence of some ethereal hellhound which, to quench its bloodthirsty nature, had slurped up the brains of its victims. According to Sanders the legend of the giant, salivating ghostly black dog had been whispered for many years, with reports stating that the beast prowled the marshes of a night in search of food. Despite a search of the area in an attempt to find the skulls, Sanders could only state, 'we found many broken coffins and hundreds of bones, but no skulls'.

Despite their fanciful resolutions as to the culprit, they came across no demonic skull-cracking hound either.

The journalists were marooned at Deadman's Island for the night, and at one point mistook wooden spikes driven into the mud at an area called Smugglers' Gut for the ghosts of slain warriors. A few hours in the thickening pea-soup fog had clearly made Sanders and Rand prone to hallucination and so with three trusty flashes of a torch, they signalled for the ferryman to return and on black waters, transport them to safety.

Blue Town's Heritage Centre, situated at No. 69 High Street, was once rumoured to have been haunted by a phantom.

Members of staff have reported seeing the top half of a spirit and believe its incomplete appearance may have been connected to the alterations made to the floor levels. However, one of Blue Town's little-known reputed hauntings dates back to the early part of the twentieth century. I've always been intrigued by old newspaper reports that have been gathering dust over the years, especially as they are often written in such dramatic, convoluted fashion, so for now I'd like to share with you the story of the 'Supposed ghost at Blue Town' which appeared in the *Guardian & East Kent Advertiser* of 20 October 1906. I record the tale of the 'Strange Rattlings in the Dark' in its entirety, as follows:

Deadman's Island was said to be the prowling ground of a bloodthirsty phantom hound. (Illustration by Simon Wyatt)

Blue Town Heritage Centre.

There has been hinted abroad a rumour to the effect that on a recent night, when creepy darkness was coming on, Blue Town had a remarkable visitor in the form of a ghost, but investigations into the affair have not led to the confirmation of the report. It seems true, however, that this neighbourhood has lately experienced something out of the ordinary, but the evidence to connect this with any ghost – be it Bill Bailey's or anybody else's – is microscopic, so microscopic in fact, that it really wants a lot of detecting. Some missiles have been thrown by an unseen hand after people going down the alleys, and the good people of Blue Town – those living in the Chapel Street part of it, we mean – at once jumped to the conclusion that it was the prank of a ghost. There have been strange and disconcerting rattlings in the passages, and poor souls, it is reported, have become terribly unnerved by them. They gazed upwards intently, but failed to see any apparition flitting about the housetops. They looked all about them with piercing eyes, but no ghost confronted them. They felt no wonderful touch of a mysterious hand, and the strangeness of it all seems to have temporarily unsettled them. What could it all mean? What Machiavellian hand could have been at work?

The report continues, in suspenseful manner, stating:

Much as the disturbed folk pondered over the matter in their agitation they could only think of one thing – the ghost. They appeared to have become too superstitious to attribute the hideous rattlings on the stone to the work of anything else but a ghost. But this story about the Blue Town ghost has proved to be all a myth, and only existed in the imagination of the people. We do imagine strange things sometimes, especially when the liver is out of condition! But listen to what rumour spread. It is an amusing story and must be taken with the proverbial pinch of salt. Rumour circulated it about that this apparition was fairly playing 'high jink' with the denizens of Blue Town, startling them out of their wits almost. They became possessed with strange feelings, wondering what mad prank the ghost would be up to next. Old women trembled like an aspen leaf and point blank refused to leave the innermost part of their homes until some self-possessed soul, after much effort, succeeded in persuading them that there was no danger in venturing out.

'Why, bless me,' this kindly person is declared to have said. 'I've been out and about as usual and no ghost has come up to me.' Such words as these are enough to make anybody take fresh courage and they are reported to have had a sort of magical influence over these frightened old women. The smiles which had previously credited them with happy-looking faces returned and their countenances beamed again with old-time radiancy! They ventured out once more but this time with a suspicion of timidity which suggested that the ghost had not entirely left their minds. But lo! The poor creatures soon had their peace of mind disturbed again. One of them, on venturing out as above stated, decided to take advantage of the opportunity of doing a bit of shopping. Rumour says that,

Chapel Street, Blue Town.

among other articles she purchased some tinned meat (whether American or not rumour does not tell us) for the 'old man's supper'. She started hurrying home with it, and on proceeding down the entry leading to the back of her home a quantity of oyster shells followed in her wake. They were, it is said, hurled down the passage with sufficient force to set up a startling noise. They seemed to have startled the poor woman, anyhow, for rumour says down went 'hubby's' supper on to the cold stone, and indoors rushed the wife, considerably frightened. But who aimed the oyster shells?

And so to the gripping conclusion!

That was a mystery at the time but it has since been cleared up. Then rumour has told us that other people in Blue Town have met with a similar experience, the only exception being that stones were thrown in their cases instead of oyster shells, the ghost having probably run out of the latter? Such then is the pretty story told by rumour. But rumour is wrong about the ghost for despite the untiring observations of all the quidaunes who assembled on the spot and kept careful vigil not the least sign of a ghost presented itself to them. Moreover it has since been ascertained that all this throwing of oyster shells and stones was the work, not of a ghost, but a real, living man out for a lark, a foolish lark no doubt. He concealed himself from view, and as people entered the passage he hurled the missiles after them and so startled the people. But his game has now been stopped. The Blue Townites are now in their normal state of composure and so ends the story of the pseudo-ghost.

Sadly (despite the suspense), a not-so spellbinding conclusion after all, but Sheerness still has its fair share of unexplainable events. Another reputedly haunted building located at Blue Town is the Royal Fountain Hotel, which has been turned into flats and can be found on West Street. The building was constructed in 1807 and often catered for wealthy visitors to the town, as well as army and naval officers. The *Sheppey Gazette* of 9 December 1982 announced that, 'Lord Nelson's love nest is up for sale', commenting that the hotel 'dates back to the seventeenth century' and was 'rebuilt in 1727', although a blue plaque on the wall in Blue Town High Street states otherwise. The building ceased trading as a hotel in the early 1980s but was always said to have been 'used as a secret meeting place by Lord Nelson and Lady Hamilton'. If the building was erected in 1807 (as stated on the plaque) this is unlikely, as Nelson died two years previously, in 1805. However, there may have been another coaching inn on the site previously – possibly called The Fountain. The report added that 'the hotel was given its royal name after a visit by George II to the dockyard when he occupied a suite of rooms'.

Nelson was said to have stayed at the hotel whilst waiting for one of his ships to be repaired. According to the paper, 'in one of the rooms is a cot-bed used by Nelson on board H.M.S. *Victory*' whilst in a neighbouring room, a four-poster bed which was once used by Lady Hamilton at her Queenborough residence was also added. At the time of its operation, the hotel attracted a number of visitors, many whom stayed the night in these beds. A former landlord named Alf Sheppard told the newspaper that,

Blue Town High Street.

'they are the two most used bedrooms in the hotel. Everybody likes to sleep in Nelson's bed. It's a lovely bed. I've tried it myself.'

Sadly the hotel couldn't merely survive on legends and it's unlikely the alleged spirits still linger. The guesthouse has a spooky past, with several mentions years ago of weird noises and fleeting shadows; a chap who lived behind the hotel stated quite categorically that there was something untoward about the whole building. He mentioned that on occasion he'd heard the sound of a baby crying and that the stairs were often frequented by a woman dressed in old-fashioned clothing. Other residents in the block reported waking up in the dead of night, only to be greeted by the figure of a man standing at the end of their bed. The figure never reacts to those rousing from their slumber and after a short while fades slowly into nothing. Other rumours have circulated that a spirit, allegedly to have originated from the early eighteenth century, makes itself known in one of the flats by pottering about in an invisible kitchen and making itself a cup of tea. In 1978 Alf Sheppard and Olè Kuhlmann were partners in running the hotel. At the time Alf and Olè were keen to bring a bit of history back to Blue Town and felt that the hotel was a perfect way of keeping the past alive. Their aims were highlighted in the 29 September edition of the *Sheerness Times Guardian*, although their plans to 'put the Royal Fountain back on the map' sadly didn't work out. Even so, Alf was all too keen to promote the ghostly activity, commenting that, 'guests have sworn to the existence of something. Whether faulty door catches or sash chords are to

The Royal Fountain Hotel. It has since been converted to flats.

blame, noises have been heard.' Perhaps as a precaution, the newspaper added, 'any wandering spirit would find a welcome in the winding corridors, the cobbled yard, bathrooms and kitchens. He or she is friendly!'

Mr Kuhlmann was a tad more sceptical regarding the alleged wraith, but did mention that if such a spook were evident, then he would not be afraid of it. More than thirty years previous to Mr Sheppard and Kuhlmann's ownership, a woman named Gwen claimed to have had a frightening experience with the reputed spectre. She commented how the spirit was very real, saying, 'Believe me, there is one, I've seen him,' and that 'the ghost made my blood run cold'. Gwen had been staying at the Royal Fountain in the 1950s when her encounter took place. She stated:

It was more than thirty years ago when the clanking of his chains and the slamming of a car door heralded his arrival. He came into my room in a blinding white light. All around him was light illuminating his gaunt features which were heavily bandaged. He was tall and slim and came across the floor towards me and stopped stock still – just stood there with his arms folded – and disappeared as quickly as he came.

Gwen reported how some of her friends worked at the hotel as maids. They lived in the attic rooms and would often dare each other to frequent the ill-lit corridors and if brave enough, to spend just a few short moments in Lord Nelson's bed. However, when Gwen stayed in the room, strange things began to happen.

She explained, 'Everything moved – the bed, tables, chairs – everything, and it was not imagination. I'll swear to it.'

It was shortly after this bout of weird activity that Gwen had her actual sighting of the spectre, although she couldn't grasp the meaning of it. She continued:

None of it made sense. The clanking of chains and the car door were out of sequence in time. The car was too modern for this man of another age, but the sounds came together. I swear I saw him. I've had my leg pulled about it and people have made game of me suggesting it was my imagination. I think he's probably some unhappy spirit – perhaps a murderer or the victim. History books tell of a great deal of smuggling from the pier to the hotel. Who knows? One thing's for sure, he's never harmed anyone.

The Red Lion is another reputedly haunted pub. It can be found at No. 61 High Street, Blue Town and is said to be the oldest pub in the area dating back to the late 1700s, once listed as The Swan Inn. It was rumoured to have been haunted by a 'lady of the night' who plied her trade at Sheerness docks. The ghostly woman was said to have been accompanied by an equally spectral dog. A team of ghost hunters who investigated the pub claimed that they heard phantom footsteps on the landing, whilst several members reported an overwhelming feeling of dizziness and sickness, as if they were onboard a boat.

The Britannia Hotel used to sit at No. 75 High Street, Sheerness. Although it closed its doors in 1990 – it has since been taken over by a number of shops and solicitors – there are those who still recall their ghostly encounters.

The Red Lion pub.

A Mrs Beryl Kingsnorth wrote to the *Sheppey Gazette* in February 1997 with her memories. She commented:

I worked there as a barmaid from 1978 to 1980. I know very little of its earlier history except that it was originally a very fine hotel, attracting high ranking officers from the ships that came to the Royal Naval Dockyard. To me it seemed to be two pubs in one because the public bar was always very lively and popular with local people and the saloon bar was the favourite haunt of the seamen who came from the boats in the docks. My strongest memories however, are of the stories I was told about the ghosts which were supposed to roam around the cellar and the top floor. Whether one believes in them or not, there is no doubt that quite often the beer would stop flowing and upon investigation the landlord found that the gas taps had been turned off. One can only surmise that the ghost was either teetotal or just a spoilsport.

Although Beryl never actually experienced anything troublesome at the Britannia, she was certainly in fear of the rumours; she added:

One evening in particular, I remember. The landlord had to go out and said he would not be back in time to open up, so would I do it? I didn't fancy the idea much but didn't like to refuse and so it was with great trepidation that I arrived there. It was dark and I had to unlock the door to the public bar in Rose Street, which meant that I had to walk through the bar to reach the light switches. Having done that and already feeling nervous I then had to go upstairs to the office to bring down the tills. I could only carry one at a time because they were quite heavy and there were three of them. By the time I had done the journey three times I was absolutely terrified although I never saw or heard anything untoward. Imagination can be a wonderful, but also a terrible thing!

The Victory pub, which was originally located on Victory Street and later moved to Railway Road in Sheerness, made headlines in 1991 when the Warne family temporarily moved in to manage the Railway Road premises. 'Ghostly Goings On Haunt Pub Family' was the headline the *Sheerness Times Guardian* ran on 31 January 1991 in reference to the family's introduction to the festive peculiarities. According to the paper, 'the couple [Dennis and Cynthia, accompanied by their sons, 19-year-old Adam and 8-month-old Christopher] arrived at the Shepherd Neame pub just before Christmas … and it wasn't long before they noticed that there was something "different" about the place'.

Like a number of witnesses to paranormal activity, the Warnes were initially very sceptical in regards to a possible haunting, despite hearing rumours from locals that the building had been ghost infested for a number of years. Dennis commented, 'I've never really taken any notice of this sort of thing; like everybody else I'm too busy worrying about the land of the living.'

However, as soon as the family moved in strange things began to occur. Dennis went on, '… pictures started flying off nails in the wall … there have been many times we have heard noises and seen things we cannot explain'.

Former site of the Britannia Hotel with the Clock Tower in foreground

One night in early January baby Christopher was asleep upstairs and the rest of the family were downstairs when suddenly they heard noises, as if furniture was being thrown about in the room above them. 'We ran upstairs as quickly as we could,' claimed Cynthia, 'but when we got to the study there wasn't a sign of anything.'

Whether by coincidence, the former landlord, a chap named Mike Docherty, stated that whilst he and his wife were moving items out of the pub – they were leaving for another pub in Ashford – they returned to the room and found that the carpet had been rolled up all ready for the removal van!

Those who knew of the peculiar happenings at the pub often spoke about how the unsettled spirit could well be that of an ex-landlord who committed suicide on the premises many years ago.

The name of the man was Arthur, but was it him who was responsible for tampering with the pumps? Cynthia said:

> On Christmas Eve we were convinced that we had run out of coke and lemonade. The pump wasn't bringing anything up from the cellar so we used bottles all over Christmas. When Dennis went down to the cellar, though, he discovered that the gas cylinder had been physically turned off. We are the only ones to go down there and we are absolutely certain that neither of us had done that.

Just a short distance from Railway Road is Clyde Street. No. 55 is the site of the Blacksmiths Arms, which at the time of writing stands empty. In June 2013 Kent Online reported that landlord Mark Hughes had applied for permission to convert the pub into two terraced houses and a ground-floor flat. In the 1980s there was much talk of a ghostly presence at the pub. The occupiers then were Kevin and Mo Beddows who, up until 1986, experienced a number of uncanny incidents – but then the spectre left as quickly as it had arrived. Mo reported, 'It was as real as any apparition can be – a presence to be reckoned with – a spirit who would silently move bottles around the bar and in the cellar.'

Reputed pub ghosts always seem to spend much of their time in those damp cellars – ideal habitats, one would assume, for something so unearthly. The couple also reported the usual unnatural chills which they took as a sign that the presence was near. However, the Beddows believed that it was in fact their fault that the ghost disappeared. Mo added,

'… he was harmless enough and we ousted him without realising it when the pub had a face-lift. What with all the alterations – including the conversion of a terrace house to create a pool and darts area – he just took off.'

Meanwhile, the ghost of a little boy was once said to haunt Halfway Houses Primary School situated on Southdown Road. The school used to be known as Halfway Primary, and part of it dates back to 1910. Betty Oldmeadow was the secretary there for more than twenty years. She commented, 'I spoke to some retired teachers who used to work at Halfway School and they remembered a rumour about the old air-raid shelter there being haunted'. However, the young boy phantom appears to be a separate entity and it is believed that he fell ill and died but possibly still frequents the place.

The Blacksmiths Arms on Clyde Street.

I was also contacted by a chap named Philip who told me several ghost stories related to Sheerness. He commented:

As a little boy I always grew up knowing and hearing stories from family and friends about ghosts etc. When I was young my parents told me about the time they were walking in the alleyways of Maple Street one evening [around 1965] while they were courting (their words) and trying to have that sneaky kiss when my dad saw what he thought was a sheet blow over the wall. My dad in his day would nick [steal] anything, as most young-sters would! So he jumped on the wall to get the sheet to take home. However the sheet seemed to disappear into the house. My parents were both startled by this so walked fast round to the front of the house where there was a lady sitting around a table calling in the spirits. They were both scared but they always disbelieved what they saw so much so that when they recall this story they say 'but we don't believe it'.

Philip continued:

A fair few years previous to this [presumably in the early 1960s] my mum was babysitting for a family in the same road [possibly in the same house]. There were flowers in a vase on the table and the water in the vase kept turning to blood! This 'water' was tested and proven to be blood. The story was covered by local media and some of the major tabloids! My mum was very freaked out by this but since then is always reluctant to speak about it, often stating that 'yeah, maybe it happened'.

A few years later, Philip had been living at Wellesley Road in Sheerness and his neighbours, a big family, were a bright and cheerful lot until they moved to Maple Street. One wintry day Philip visited his ex-neighbours to give them a Christmas card, but, according to Philip, there was 'a very strange feeling of nastiness from the house. The dog was scratching at the door and the family were no longer bright and cheerful.'

Philip, although still a youngster, rushed home to his parents and told them how he'd felt uneasy but couldn't really explain the peculiar atmosphere and attitude of the family. He added: 'A few months later our friends had packed up and moved and the house was boarded. Later that year the family's story was in the paper that they had moved away as their house was haunted by a ghost of a cat and a man in Victorian attire who took over the house. The house was later sold but this took many years.'

I was extremely intrigued by this haunted house tale, but found another equally terrifying example in the *Sheerness Times Guardian* of 1 May 1981 under the heading, 'Terror Spirit Stalks Hope St. Home'. A Sheerness resident claimed to have been 'paralysed' with fear after encountering paranormal activity. According to the report, 37-year-old Margaret Parsons had fallen 'victim to evil spirits' on the Saturday night previous and had remained in bed 'unwilling to talk or eat', according to her brother. The report continued that, 'Today (Friday) she has an appointment to visit her doctor and her family hope she can be persuaded to overcome her terror.' Margaret's brother, Andy Ralph, and his wife Julie, who were in their late teens at the time, told the newspaper

Maple Street – an unlikely setting for a ghost story?

that Margaret had visited their home at Hope Street on the Saturday and had come face to face with the ghost of a man described as being about 50 years of age, wearing glasses and dressed in a pinstripe suit. When Margaret saw the spirit she, according to her brother, 'appeared to be in a trance and kept saying, "get it out". We were terrified. We all fled and there is no way we will ever go back to that place. Never.'

The teenage couple had been aware of a peculiar presence in the house since that January and other relatives and friends had heard strange noises in the property but it was only Margaret who came face to face with the wraith. Despite the chilly encounter her husband Ron told the paper that 'she remembers nothing of the experience … her eyes were bloodshot and when I looked into her eyes it was as though I was sharing the experience.'

The *Times Guardian* added that, 'the Ralphs, who have a seven-month-old daughter say they were fortunate to have experienced nothing more sinister than odd coins being thrown around a room, doors shutting themselves; a feeling of being watched and lights switched on and off.' According to the paper the weirdness began on 6 January with Andy commenting, 'I can pinpoint the date exactly because it was Twelfth Night and I had taken down Christmas decorations. From then on it's been uncanny.'

The family investigated the history of the property and discovered that a middle-aged man had lived alone in the flat and died in 1974 from pneumonia. A neighbour stated that the man's name was Harry and that he was a quiet man, so it seemed a big mystery as to why the spirit – if it was that of the deceased gentleman – appeared to cause

Hope Street – the former site of a haunted house.

so much mischief. The same neighbour commented that, 'I've never been aware of anything evil in the house and I've lived here a good many years. There are empty buildings either side and it's possible that cats or rats could roam around making odd noises. It's all very strange.'

A spiritualist lady named Florence Grounsell was of the opinion that Margaret Parsons may have been unknowingly receptive to spirits and told the newspaper, 'I would need her co-operation and that of everyone else who was in the house at the time to help drive out the spirits with the cross and prayer, but they are unwilling to return to the house.'

The teenage couple and their daughter were so troubled by the alleged spiritual encounter that they stayed at the house of Margaret and her husband, Ron, until they could find another flat. However, the following week a Broad Street resident wrote to the newspaper with his take on the alleged haunting, stating:

Sir – All compassionate people will feel the utmost sympathy for the plight of the residents of the house in Hope Street – For so long in the history of mankind, such odd happenings, which at first seem attributable only to the presence of evil spirits or some allied supranormal cause, upon careful investigation result in a completely rational explanation. If we set our feet firmly on the ground and recognise that there is no such thing as the supernatural we shall have made a good start. People believe what they want to believe, that is why so many resort to so-called psychic mediums or the ritual of religious exorcism with a crucifix and holy water to deal with those demons.

The sceptical enquirer was certainly quick to debunk the possibility of a ghostly figure prowling the Hope Street property, and like that equally dismissive neighbour agreed that, 'Perhaps a loose

The view down Hope Street.

floorboard or a broken hinge might show the cause of what they imagine is the presence of evil spirits.' The Broad Street resident concluded:

> In the two chapters entitled 'The omnipresence of demons', and 'The expulsion of embodied evils', in his monumental work, *The Golden Bough*, Sir James Frazer sets out the amazing catalogues of magical rituals and religious incantations employed by priests and magicians to exorcise evil spirits. The neighbours of the troubled residents in Hope Street, who said: 'There are empty buildings on either side and it's possible that rats or cats could roam around making odd noises,' is almost certainly on the right.

Despite his theories, the author of the letter failed to explain the entity that Margaret Parsons had reputedly encountered and, judging by local gossip, others had experienced the same activity.

Mr Frost's Chilly Encounter ...

In July 2013 I was contacted by a Bob Frost, a Sheppey resident who was keen to speak of a weird encounter he had had a few decades previously. He wrote:

> It was 1966 and I was employed as deckhand on the Trinity House pilot cutters in Sheerness docks. We operated as two man crews, deckhand and cox, on shifts covering 24/7, 365 days a year, based in an office that still sits on the sea wall near Garrison Point Fort. The fort lies at the end of dock road and the road has a high wall running down its length with the working docks inside.

Sheerness docks – this way for ghosts!

The office has a clear view looking down at the road and wall, and at that time there was a building used as the customs and excise offices alongside the road. It was the early hours of the morning and we had a slack shift and I was feeling peckish so decided that tea and toast was called for. Our office building had a fully functional kitchen but the toaster was a bit fierce and my toast burnt. I stood at the sink scratching the burnt bits off my toast when, through the window, out of the corner of my eye I caught a movement. Coming down the road, partially shielded by some trees, appeared to be someone in a white raincoat heading towards the customs building. As they got closer I realised that the lights on the road had gone out automatically at 01:00 hrs and I shouldn't be able to see anyone in the dark. As the figure cleared the trees I saw what I can only describe as a tall luminous man dressed in Elizabethan clothes striding down the road. He must have been in sight for over a minute when he went behind the customs building to appear out the other side and carried on down the road. At this point I realised that he was actually walking just above the road and not on it. As he got nearer the fort he disappeared through the wall into the area of the dry dock. By this time I had dropped my toast and it took a few seconds to get myself back into mode.

I went into the office and told the cox that I had just seen a ghost. He didn't bat an eyelid. 'Son,' he said, 'I've seen hundreds of them down here.'

Site of Sheerness docks.

Shortly after this I left Trinity House to join the merchant navy. Roll the clock on to 1993 and I found myself back in the docks on security. In an idle moment I was recounting my tale to my workmates when one told me that a guy on the other shift had reported seeing a ghost come through the wall while he was patrolling the dry dock. I spent many hours patrolling the docks on night shift but never saw anything else, but always had a sense of peaceful contentment whilst being there. At the time of the incident Sheerness docks was in the period between the naval dockyard having closed and the commercial docks really taking off with a ferry terminal etc. On a personal basis I was young and fit, having just left the army, and drink was taboo at work and drugs taboo period. I can describe what I saw but don't know what it was. Was it a replay from the past? A lost soul perhaps? I just know what I saw and the fact that I was fascinated but not frightened.

Another naval encounter of the ghostly type was said to have taken place in the late 1700s when Britain were at war with the French. Sheerness docks were extremely busy at the time as Britain was in need of great ships, but one morning, as Sheila M. Judge writes, '… there were to be heard sounds in the air of a nature well known to the ears of the many old salts who then dwelt in the town'. It was said that the cacophony was of some 'heavy naval engagement' taking place not far away and that so many men were put on guard as the booming echoed across the sky from over the horizon. However, much to the bemusement of those on guard, there was to be no attack; instead it seemed that those on alert had witnessed some type of ghostly battle but alas, no, the sounds emanating from the sea were simply heavy, iron water tanks being struck by the strong gales, causing a booming effect. At Garrison Point Fort, situated within the docks, there is talk of an old ghostly tale which is attached to the dockyard church. Many years ago there was a rumour of several sightings of an eerie figure being seen hanging from one of the trees in front of the church. Those unfortunate enough to encounter the hanging spectre spoke of how there was never any rope visible, but merely a dangling wraith floating in mid-air under the stark branches.

Psychic medium Mia Dolan, who is mentioned in the Minster segment, had a creepy encounter whilst living in a flat with family in a residential close inside the docks. At the time she was in her mid-teens. It was a pleasant morning when Mia exited the top-floor flat with her elder brother's friend, but as they closed the front door behind them they heard the most horrifying scream. Both shocked, they peered over the stairwell in time to see a young boy tumbling down the stone steps, hitting the bottom with a crunch. Within a few moments Mia and her friend were within several feet of the boy, who suddenly disappeared into thin air.

There had been no sign whatsoever of the incident, and not a trace of the boy. Shortly afterwards, so intrigued by what they both had witnessed, Mia visited the Sheerness department of births and deaths but could find no mention of the boy. When she visited the library situated at Sheerness, however, she came across something which shocked her to the core. A young boy had been killed at Blue Town by falling down a set of steps some fifty years before. An even more staggering detail was the fact that it had happened on 21 January, the same date Mia and her friend had witnessed the tumbling apparition.

From then on Mia began to realise that she had become a person sensitive to such spirits and energies. She would begin to hear messages in her head, warning her of things about to occur. Mia now gives psychic readings and is a best-selling author.

The docks have long been considered haunted. A resident of Sheerness once reported that:

View towards Garrison Point.

A friend of mine's father was a petty-officer in the war – attached to submarines – but he spent most of his time diving. Unfortunately one of the things he had to do was dive and get into a submarine that had gone down off the Isle of Sheppey, where all hands were lost. He had to break into this submarine, locate all the dead bodies and bring them to the surface and off to funerals and so on.

It's sometimes said that the shadowy figures seen around the docks on certain nights are these restless souls who perished onboard those submarines, although areas where waiting sailors used to hang their hammocks could also explain some of the peculiar shadows of a night. A chap named Peter once recalled how, 'along the walls [of the docks] there are hundreds of enormous eyes – like hooks and eyes – where sailors waiting for ships would stick their hammocks up'. Perhaps their energy has seeped into those granite structures, replayed back on the rare occasion to those susceptible to such things. Peter added that there are 'lots of little ghosts lurking in those places – real atmospheric places'.

Just outside the docks at Sheerness is Bridge Road. The Civil Defence Corps used to be situated here and the building was thought to have been haunted. According to a small report in the *Sheerness Times Guardian* in 1961, 'Doors have been heard to open and close. Footsteps have been heard in the passage. But nobody has been found.' Members of the building told the newspaper that the ghostly presence often makes itself known during committee meetings, with one

Bridge Road, Sheerness.

associate commenting, 'we first noticed the noises about two years ago soon after I came here. Sitting round the table at a meeting we heard the front door open then close. Footsteps went up the passage. And that's the mystery because they have yet to be heard coming back.'

The article added that the premises may well have been built on burial ground and this confirmed my suspicions when I found a small snippet of information regarding the discovery of a 150-year-old skull and other bones whilst during an excavation at Bridge Road.

The Civil Defence Corps were keen to move from their premises in the early 1960s but not because of the reputed presence. Civil Defence Chief Mr Ken Thomas stated, 'He [the ghost] has become part of the Corps now but we want better accommodation.'

Intriguingly, the following year the *Sheerness Times Guardian* of 30 November 1962 asked, 'what on earth has made George the ghost go?' after the same Civil Defence members had reported a distinct lack of activity on their premises, regarding a spirit that had now been given the name of George. The article stated that the spectre 'seems to have vanished', leaving ardent ghost-believers of the committee wondering if he'll ever return. The small snippet of information appeared in the 'Island Roundabout' column, with its author stating, 'some said in no uncertain terms that George existed. Others were more sceptical and said that a loose floor-board needed to be nailed down.' Even so, the article once again touched on the idea of the building at Bridge Road being erected on a cemetery site, with a historian claiming that the Civil Defence building 'stands on the site of a cemetery in which the bones of the victims from two ancient wars still rest'. The report concludes that 'George' could well be 'the ghost of an old warrior who is trying to get into this life to prevent war-suffering by joining the Civil Defence Corps'.

More Shivers ...

In 1989 island resident Paul Deadman met the woman who would become his wife. However, in the autumn of that year the couple had a spooky encounter at Sheerness. Paul reported:

We were walking along the beach path near the floodgate at the bottom of Beach Street one evening. My wife was wearing a knee length skirt and was messing around pulling it up to her thigh and we were laughing and joking around when she said 'Oh, I'd better stop as there's an old man there!'

I looked around and answered her but less than a few seconds later I looked back and he had disappeared! I said 'Where's he gone,' or something similar and looked up and down the beach front which was flood-lit; the flood gate was closed also and there's no way an old man could have run away that fast! The nearest steps were quite a distance away in each direction. Needless to say we left the area very quickly! As for a description we both confirmed that it was an old man wearing a flat cap and a long coat. It was a very eerie experience!

One of the weirdest ghostly encounters at Sheerness took place a number of years ago and involved a window cleaner.

Beach Street.

One afternoon a Mr Crome was cleaning the windows of a Sheerness house when suddenly, in the reflection of the pane, he saw the figure of an old man standing directly behind him. Mr Crome could see every inch and detail of the man; he estimated his height to be over 6ft and saw that the chap was wearing a collarless shirt. However, when Mr Crome spun around to greet the fellow there was nobody within sight. The eeriness didn't stop there, though. As the window cleaner descended to the basement windows he felt a terrible weight on his shoulders and became frozen with fear. Hurriedly finishing the window, Mr Crome came out of the basement and a short while after spoke to a local lady about the incident. She stated that in the past a builder, whilst perched on his ladder over the same window where Mr Crome saw

the ghostly reflection, was suddenly flung from his steps by an invisible force.

Stranger still, this hadn't been the first time the window cleaner had seen spirits in the reflections of windows, there having been similar encounters in London before.

In 1996 the Co-op branch situated on Sheerness High Street announced that it would be closing its doors. At the time of its closure it seems that the protests did not merely originate from those who would be left without jobs. A ghostly presence began to make itself known, particularly in the Wheatsheaf Hall segment of the building, and staff would state quite categorically that they were not willing to venture into the adjacent areas known as the Unity and Wellington Halls. The ghostly presence would sporadically manifest itself in the form of footsteps and odd noises and the Co-op staff would occasionally speak of an unseen manifestation that would move items around. Minster resident Betty Oldmeadow informed me:

The old Unity Hall was over the Co-op furniture shop next to the Wheatsheaf Hall at 100 High Street, Sheerness. The hall was eventually used to store furniture. There was a series of corridors that linked the buildings together, thus I was jokingly reminded about the 'ghost' when it was necessary for me to go up to a temporary office near the hall; I can't find out more about the ghost because unfortunately, most of my old colleagues from the Co-op have now passed on.

However, after a few enquiries I was contacted by a chap named Tony who told me:

In September 1986 I began work at the CWS Co-Operative Furnishing store in Sheerness High Street which is roughly where Iceland is now. In those days Health and Safety had never been heard of and so upstairs on the top floor, which was next to the Co-op hall, the remaining floor space had been turned into warehouse space. Furniture was stored in the hall, and in a room at the back of the hallway the hardware stock was stored whilst the electrical goods for the electrical department were in a separate shop further up the High Street. This room was kept under lock and key and in order to get to it you had to walk across a dark room to access the lightswitch to turn the lights on, for not only the room in which the electrical items were kept,

but the floor space you had to traverse in order to reach it. In the Christmas period of 1987, after the Co-op toy shop had closed and the remaining stock transferred to the furnishing store – also being kept upstairs – I had occasion late one afternoon when it was dark, to go to the electrical storeroom in order to check on the stock level of a certain model of TV. As I walked into the darkened area of the stockroom, having walked across a lit floor, and had begun to undo the padlock that secured the electrical stockroom door, a sudden chill came over me and I suddenly felt a cold hand clap me on the back of my shoulder. I was aware that no one else could possibly be in the warehouse with me and a chill went down my spine. Feeling very alarmed at this I rushed back downstairs to gather my wits and as I reached the shop floor it was pointed out to me that I was shivering. One of the two other men who worked there suddenly exclaimed 'Oh look, he's met Mary.'

I asked who Mary was and was told the following story … A few years earlier when the Co-op hall had still been used to host dances, one Christmas whilst locking up, Joe, who was at the time the caretaker and was now still working at the store as security, came across the body of an elderly lady who had been attending the dance there. She was at the base of a short flight of stairs. It was thought that she had been looking for her way out of the dance hall and had fallen down the stairs, which had resulted in her death. She was said since then to often reappear during the Christmas period, mainly to male staff who often reported feeling someone touching their shoulder. Joe had had several encounters with her over the years and had in the week preceding my experience been sitting upstairs in the staff room alone whilst waiting for a keep fit class that used part of the hall on a Monday night to finish up. Whilst he was sitting there [Joe was partially deaf] he felt someone clap him on the shoulder as well.

Whenever it was dark and I had to go up to the warehouse after that I would always announce myself and say 'Hello' to Mary in case she was hanging around as such. I encountered her on two further occasions after that. The first was a few weeks later whilst carrying a three-seater settee down the spiral staircase that led from the dance-hall to the hallway that separated the furnishing store and the Co-op chemist that was next door. As I reached the

bottom of the stairs – I was going backwards – I happened to glance upwards at the landing at the top of the stairs and there, to my astonishment, was an elderly lady, dressed as though she was going to a dance and quite petite. I immediately realised who it was and didn't say anything until we had finished loading the settee into a delivery van. I then went and found Joe and asked him to describe to me what Mary was wearing and looked like when he discovered her body. He described perfectly the woman that I had just seen a few minutes ago.

The final encounter with her was not a sighting but a happening that occurred in connection with her. In the winter of 1988 a few weeks before I left the Co-op several of the women who worked in the hardware department

Site of former Co-op building in Sheerness High Street.

and I were discussing Mary when all of a sudden a rack of saucepans that was fixed hanging to the shop floor collapsed and came crashing down to the floor. Upon checking the fixture there was no reason as to why it should have done this. After talking to various members of staff who worked there at the time and a friend of mine who had worked there previously and had encountered Mary, I have come to the following conclusion as to her appearance. It was always to male members of the staff and always in the winter time. I believe the reasons for this were that Mary was looking for the way out of the hall when she died and knew that there was a male member of staff on duty. The clap on my shoulder was similar to that which someone would administer to you if they were tapping you on the shoulder to get your attention in order to ask you something. I think she was still trying to find her way out of the building and was approaching male members of the staff in order to try and ask them to show her the way out. I don't know if she is still there as the Co-op shut in the '90s and was sold off as separate buildings.

Tony's theory intrigued me and was confirmed by a former warehouseman who added that at the time of the store's imminent closure:

There are so many things that are unexplained since the announcement that the stores would close. The first noises I heard were like someone in torment. Then there were sounds of footsteps, lights coming on and off, showers of new nails and nuts being hurled around and smashed mirror glass in a place where there was never a mirror.

Oddly, none of the dancers who used the Wheatsheaf Hall reported any levels of strangeness, but the warehouse operative commented:

Now there are sounds from all three halls. We hear footsteps and in the Unity Hall we were astonished to see the head of a mannequin go flying across the room. Then, for no reason, an old brass light-fitting crashed to the floor, from a ceiling where there are only strip lights. We've also ducked a well-aimed ashtray.

A psychic medium called in to help the unsettled spirit claimed that the spectre had pleaded to be left alone to roam the empty halls and also confirmed that the apparition is that of a woman named Mary. Mind you, the medium's version of Mary's death differed from Tony's: it was claimed that the woman had died after she had fallen over in the Wheatsheaf Hall and somehow become locked in the building where she suffered a heart attack.

The ghostly episodes had become so severe that on one occasion the warehouse operative, who was a keyholder at the time, had to call the police. For some unknown reason the alarm to the building had sounded but when the police left, assuring the employee everything was in order, several footsteps could be heard echoing through the building and a number of doors were also heard banging. The police returned but could find no trace of an intruder. The warehouse worker in question always considered himself a down-to-earth fellow and not the sort prone to flights of fancy, but he was quite content to tell a newspaper, 'There are times when the hair stands up on the back of my neck – there is a presence.'

Tony also told me about another ghostly encounter he experienced:

In July 1989 I was away at Hendon Police College doing my twenty weeks' basic training having just joined the Metropolitan Police Force, as it was in those days, in March of that year. As was my custom I would phone my mum on the Thursday night in order to let her know that I would be returning home for the weekend on the Friday night. That Friday I arrived at Sheerness railway station at around 5.30 p.m. and instead of walking straight home, which was in Granville Road at about the midway point, I walked into the High Street up to Viddlers newsagents at the opposite end to the railway station and picked up my weekly magazines that they reserved for me. This meant that I then walked the short distance down St Georges Avenue to enter Granville Road from that end as opposed to the Rose Street end that I would normally have accessed it from. As I got outside No. 71 I saw the elderly male resident that I was very familiar with, Mr Jenkins, stood outside his front door which, having no front garden, meant that he was on the pavement. I was close enough to reach out and touch him and said 'Hello, Mr Jenkins'. He just looked blankly at me and raised his hat that he was wearing. It was a hot day but he had on his overcoat and hat! I just shrugged my shoulders and thought, miserable old git, must be in one of his funny moods again. I walked the few yards to my house, which was ten doors away, and upon entering the living room the first thing my mum said to me was, 'Guess who died last night? – Mr Jenkins!'

I believe that as I was not aware of his death, that my mind was still receptive to his signal which is why I could see him clearly and interact with him. I believe that as the brain is made up of electrical impulses it can at times act like a radio receiver and that instead of the constant static and lack of signal that most people encounter, when atmospheric conditions are favourable and other conditions are present that we sometimes have just for a few moments or so a clear signal that we pick up. I was still on Mr Jenkins' wavelength, so to speak, which is why I saw him and no one else did.

Mai Griffin is an international artist and writer of fiction who spent some of her childhood growing up in Sheerness after her father had been posted on the island during the war. One evening in 1938 Mai had been asleep in her bedroom when her father came in to check on her. Outside the window a beautiful fat moon was hanging in the night sky and Mai's father fetched her mother so they could both observe the eerie glow. Suddenly however, Mai's mother – who had been sensitive to spirits throughout her life – noticed the apparition of her aunt Agnes who although smiling, shook her head and pointed to the clock on the mantelpiece – the hands standing at 11.30 p.m. Mai's mother looked back at the ghost of her aunt but the apparition was nowhere to be seen. She sensed, though, that this appearance was a warning of sorts. Mai's father had not seen the ghostly figure and tried to play down the apparition until the following day, when a telegram arrived from Mai's grandfather stating that his wife's uncle had passed away at 11.30 the previous night – the same time the apparition had appeared. Mai and her family were to have many strange episodes, but this was the last to occur in Sheppey before they moved to Lancashire in 1939.

A number of ghost stories may have no foundation to back up their existence, but at times there is no doubting the power of a yarn. One such tale attached to Sheerness was passed around between many youths going back over several decades and was said to have concerned an old couple who lived and worked in the town. According to legend, the elderly gentleman had a wooden leg and it was always his wish to save up as much money as he could and eventually purchase for himself a false leg made of gold. Although this took some time to achieve, he eventually saved up enough money to be able to afford this luxury golden leg. Sadly however, due to his age, the man passed away shortly afterwards and was buried with his false leg. However, after the death of her husband the woman began to struggle with the local business they had run for many years and in desperation decided that the only way she could pay the mounting bills was to exhume her husband's grave in order to obtain the golden leg, which she could sell on. One clammy night, or so the story goes, the woman visited her husband's grave and by the glare of the moon dug the soil until she retrieved the golden leg which she unscrewed from her partner's body. A few nights later, whilst sitting in bed, the woman began to feel rather ashamed by her actions but was suddenly alarmed by the creak of the back door, which suggested that someone had entered the house. At first the woman thought she must have imagined it but again came the creak.

Surely just the wind? she thought to herself until the door shut with a bang and was followed by the sound of a few thuds echoing through the kitchen. The woman, now frightened that there might be an intruder in the house, could only remain quiet under her bedsheets as the thudding took to the stairs.

Thud! Thud! Thud! up each wooden step until the noise reached the bedroom door.

'Who's got my golden leg?' A voice snarled in question near the door, leaving the woman a tremor as she realised it was the spirit of her dead husband.

'Who's got my golden leg?' The spectre repeated in frustration, and then opened the bedroom door.

The woman peeked over the top of her sheets in horror at the sight of her ghastly gaunt husband, who, bereft of limb, approached the bed – his face screwed up in the dim light and the thud of his one remaining leg ceasing as he reached the bedside. And with that the despicable wraith boomed, 'You've got my golden leg,' and with a gnarled, dirty finger pointed at his widow …

The ending of course is down to the storyteller, but one can't argue that it's one of those spooky legends, probably passed down through generations, and that has stood to the test of time due to its vague yet eerie nature. One can imagine schoolchildren huddled around a flickering log fire at Halloween, keen to spin this wild tale of vengeance from the grave!

Another ghostly tale from Sheerness concerns small premises situated just off the main High Street on the Broadway. At the time of writing it operates as a women's clothes shop called Youwomen, but back in the 1990s the building, at No. 18, housed Threshers (a convenience store selling alcohol, wine and certainly a spirit or two).

Youwomen – formerly Threshers, at Broadway, Sheerness.

In October of 2013 I spoke to a Sheppey resident who worked at the store in the early 1990s. She told me:

I originally come from London but have lived on the island almost forty years and whilst working at Threshers heard that at some point in the past the building had been a bakery which harboured a cafe at the rear. There were always strange stories attached to the place when I was there and customers would often come into the shop and remark upon the nice smells, as if something was being baked or toasted, even though we never sold toast or cakes etc. Then the delivery men who used to bring the alcohol often commented how they were too afraid to go downstairs into the cellar area. The toilets were down there and the men, even if they needed to go to the loo, wouldn't use ours because they said there was some 'thing' down there. Other female members of staff reported sensing a presence and one of the women would always find it impossible to turn the alarms off in the shop and so she'd have to phone me at home and I'd have to come into the store.

Originally, when I began speaking to the woman, I thought this was just going to be another case of odd bumps in the night and phantom smells until she matter-of-factly told me about the day she finally witnessed the resident spectre:

Around 1992 or '93 I saw the ghost, and it was that of an old lady garbed in a waitress-type uniform – a black dress with a white pinny and small white hat of sorts. I saw her on the stairs going down to the cellar and toilet area. I was the only person to actually see this figure and I wish I'd asked her who she was and why she was there but it's the last thing you think of when you happen to come across a ghost! Around eight years later the store closed but I heard that the hairdressing staff who worked in the salon that opened upstairs had experienced a few odd things too. I also recall that the ghostly presence didn't seem to like my female boss at the time and on one occasion she was pushed across the room by an unseen assailant.

I was so fascinated by this reputedly haunted building that I visited Youwomen during mid-October 2013 and I was made very welcome by owner Michelle Gobbi, who told me that the store did indeed have a ghost and that it was still up to its old tricks. She commented:

I've been at this store about thirteen years and there's been numerous bouts of activity such as exploding light bulbs, items going missing, objects falling off shelves and a strong smell of toast. There appears to be a presence downstairs too; on one occasion a woman was in the shop with her small daughter and the young girl began talking to someone although there was no one there.

This wasn't the first time that Michelle had experienced the paranormal though. She was quick to add:

I lived at Naval Terrace at Blue Town for just a couple of years with my husband and on several occasions I saw a fleeting form out of the corner of my eye in the kitchen area, which was in the basement. It was dark in colour and either a small child or an animal but it always seemed to be flitting across an adjacent room. It took me a while to tell my husband about what I'd experienced and then found out he'd seen the same thing too. We didn't stay in the house very long, mainly because it was too big, although one night my young son began crying in his room and when I went to his aid he was standing looking out towards the window as if speaking to someone. It was a big house but it didn't feel right to me.

Michelle never did find out what exactly was haunting the Georgian building but regardless, No. 6 Naval Terrace always gave her the creeps.

For a short moment I'd like to return to the Broadway to speak of a haunted hotel. The Royal Hotel can be found at No. 29, just a stone's throw away from Michelle's store. The grand-looking hotel dates back to the early nineteenth century and was formerly known as Kent House when it operated as a pub. There are said to be a number of ghosts residing at the hotel, including an elderly lady who frequents a certain sofa upstairs and a batch of spirits, some of them ghostly children, in the cellar.

It's fair to say that you'd expect a number of old buildings to give off the occasional creak and groan, but in the *Sheerness Times Guardian* of 26 August 1960 there was a report in reference to a peculiar set of noises

Naval Terrace – No. 6 was thought to be haunted.

at Sheerness. The story appeared under the heading 'Things That Go Bump in the Night and the Day' with mention of two teenagers named Andrew Potts and Brian Finch who had contacted the newspaper to speak of a tormenting sound which often reverberated around the house of Andrew's parents. The residence, situated on Coates Avenue, was being plagued by 'queer noises' that had been experienced since the Easter of 1960. When asked what the strange noises sounded like, the teenagers responded, 'We're no scientists but so far as we can make out, the noises are static with a 50-cycle hum and the house seems to receive them rather like a guitar string. Things like doors and windows are affected, and they vibrate quite noticeably.'

Some suggestions put forward at the time included machinery being operated not far from the house that may have caused such disturbances, and yet investigations revealed nothing that would give off such a peculiar cacophony. Andrew added, 'It doesn't worry me much but our next door neighbours are very bothered with it. They say it keeps them awake.'

The newspaper article concluded that, 'A guess has been hazarded that only people with ultra-sensitive hearing can pick up the vibrations, and yet Brian stated quite categorically that people standing outside the house have heard the mysterious vibrations too.' Oddly, the noises were said to have been more frequent during the weekends but it seemed unlikely that such vibrations

The Royal Hotel.

were connected with the house; as Brian noted, 'They seem to come from the west …'

Such mysterious hums and drones have been reported throughout Britain for many years, resulting in witnesses having to move premises after getting no explanation from authorities. Whether such irritating sounds can be blamed on spirits no one is sure, but if some type of clandestine operation is taking place elsewhere in the country and causing such distractions, then maybe it could also be responsible for some of those 'haunted houses' in which occupants claim that pictures, mirrors etc. are falling off the walls of their own accord and items of furniture are moving across the room.

2

MYSTERIOUS MINSTER

The marshes which back onto the town of Minster are said to stretch towards the centre of the island, nearing Sheppey's highest point. The actual centre of the island was once marked by an old tree that fell down in 1915. The name of Minster is said to derive from the monastery founded in the area. To avoid confusion with the town of Minster-in-Thanet, Minster is often called Minster-on-Sea or Minster-in-Sheppey and was mentioned in Charles Dickens' work *The Old Curiosity Shop*. In Minster can be found the Abbey Church of the Blessed Virgin Mary and Saint Sexburgha, which was founded in AD 664 by Queen Sexburgha. According to the Sheppey Website, 'The Abbey itself is built in the centre of a former Druid or pre Druid place of worship.' This site is marked by three ancient wells, whose waters are said to aid fertility. It was historian Augustus A. Daley who wrote, 'The Isle of Sheppey, moreover, and in particular Minster-on-Sea, in the dim vista of dark and bygone ages, has played an important part, worthy in every respect, to be recorded in the pages of history.'

In 1999 a Minster woman claimed that she was attacked by a giant bird whilst she was riding her horse in the vicinity of Mill Hill. She told a local newspaper, 'It's the most bizarre and frightening experience. I was thrown and the horse bolted ... the bird had an enormous wingspan.'

The Face on the Wall

In 2012 I gave a talk on the Isle of Sheppey to a Women's Institute group. Whilst at the meeting I was shown a newspaper cutting with a photograph that had been taken at the Isle of Sheppey Academy on Minster Road. The article, posted on Halloween 2012, was featured under the headline, 'Freaked out by ghostly face on wall', and appeared to show the form of a face next to a stairwell. The image was snapped by a Lisa Gransden, who had been attending a school reunion at what was formerly the Lady Anne Cheyne School. The woman in question had been taking a tour of the buildings and was taking several photographs on the site but didn't notice the unusual manifestation until she had returned home. Lisa was spooked by the appearance of what seemed to be a face, commenting, 'I have shown it to people and everyone says it looks like a face'. But why should there be such an apparition in that area? Well, according to Lisa, 'apparently a boy fell through the roof at the school and died some time ago – I don't know how true that is though'.

Sadly, the photograph hadn't reproduced well in the newspaper but the original image most certainly seemed to show a face superimposed upon the wall.

The Ghoul of the Gatehouse

Minster Gatehouse, constructed between 1123 and 1139, now functions as a museum and can be found on Union Road. It is all that remains of a magnificent monastery and over the years may have even been used as a jail. The building was said to sport two gargoyles, used to ward off evil spirits. Rather contradictory, when you consider that some believe that the building was once used by those involved in the darker arts. It seems also that these gargoyle deterrents do not seem to have worked; for many years people have

Freaked out by ghostly face on wall

CAN you spot the uninvited guest to a school reunion in this photo?

Lisa Gransden was one of dozens of former Lady Anne Cheyne school pupils who went to the reunion on Saturday and believes one of her photos has captured a ghost.

The 45-year-old was taking a tour of the buildings at what is now the Isle of Sheppey Academy's west site in Jefferson Road, Sheerness, and was snapping away at sights which brought back memories.

When she returned home and looked through her photos from the day, she was "freaked out" to see the face on the brickwork.

The mum-of-two, of Barton Hill Drive, Minster, said: "I have shown it to people and everyone says it looks like the face. Apparently a boy fell through the roof at the school and died some time ago - I don't know how true that is though."

"It's quite scary and I do think it's a ghost. This has really freaked me out."

■ What do you think? Email timesguardian@ thekmgroup.co.uk or write to us at 44 High Street, Sheerness.

■ For more on the reunion, see page 14.

A ghost which appeared in a photo taken by Lisa Gransden

The Sheerness Times Guardian *from Halloween 2012 showing the 'ghostly face on the wall' as mentioned in the Minster segment.*

Minster Abbey Gatehouse Museum on Union Road.

mentioned a grey lady said to wander around the gatehouse. A few years ago I conducted a ghostly talk in the gatehouse for Halloween – the perfect setting for a spooky tale or two – and a number of people spoke about the figure of a woman (some believed it to be a nurse or a nun) said to walk the premises. Roger Betts, resident of Sheppey and former employee at the gatehouse commented:

I spent lots of hours in the Gatehouse both during the day and at night and never had any personal experiences of ghosts, but I heard lots of tales. I will say that when I was in there, often on my own, there was always a friendly atmosphere to the place. The Grey Lady story I heard involved a lady in a full length petticoated [*sic*] dress walking up the steps alongside the Highlanders, crossing the road and walking up the path to the church. I did have a lady visitor one day, with her husband, who I was showing around and she suddenly stopped and said 'Have you ever had any happenings here?'

I said 'No, why?' and she said 'Someone just spoke to me; a voice said "Hello Master."' We decided that the reason she was called master may have been because she was wearing trousers.

There seems to be some confusion as to whether the reputed ghost of the gatehouse is in grey or white attire. Sheila M. Judge, in *Strange Tales of Old Sheppey*, writes that with Henry VIII in power 'the nuns were driven away and most of the monastic buildings quickly given short thrift', but that 'since this traumatic event, as the villagers of old would tell,

49

the spirits of the banished nuns have wandered nightly about the site of their former home', accompanied by a phantom prioress who in life 'had been notable for her great piousness and devotion' but now seems forever in limbo haunting the site. Even so, psychic medium and Sheppey resident Mia Dolan, who is well known for her appearances on ITV's *Haunted Homes* series, once told the *Kent Messenger* of her eerie experience at Minster Gatehouse. The encounter had been her first-ever paranormal experience, and she was just 13 at the time. It was a summer evening and Mia had been attending a youth disco which was held every Monday night at around 6.00 p.m. Mia decided to walk through the grounds of the abbey to get some chips and upon returning saw a woman dressed in white standing near what she often called the Wishing Well Gate. At first Mia thought that the woman in question had been dressed for a party, but as she approached to within 30yds, the figure vanished. Mia told the newspaper, 'I was so shocked. I went back into the disco and said I'd just seen this person vanish and they all said, "Oh yeah, yeah."'

Mia believed that the ghostly figure was a nun and this may have been confirmed by a Mr and Mrs Waters, who in the 1970s were taking a daytime stroll around the gatehouse when they saw a ghostly woman who walked straight through the gate in front of them and disappeared. However, despite the sightings, others argue that there is a more complex explanation for this woman in pale dress. Brian Slade of the Sheppey Archaeological Society was, according to author Cassandra Eason, '... led to uncover legendary treasures and a host of artefacts dating back to the Bronze Age by the personage he describes as the White Lady'.

Mr Slade, after extensive research, revealed a trio of wells in the surrounding area of the gatehouse. The area was believed to have sat on a ley line (ley lines are rumoured to be ancient trackways which run across the landscape joining certain sites of historical and geographical interest), with Slade's research based on theories made in the 1950s by author Robert Goodsall, who published details of the Minster Abbey ley line, said to stretch across Kent, ending its course in the neighbouring county of Sussex. The ley line was said to have passed right through three ancient wells on the island and end at Minster. According to Slade, there may have been an ancient stone structure similar to Stonehenge, but this

Beware of the gatehouse ghouls!

was destroyed by St Sexburgha's husband and the stones were used to build the current building. According to Eason, 'The large boulder at the Abbey entrance, embedded in the wall of the King's Arms public house in Minster, is said to be all that remains of the ancient temple.'

Brian Slade excavated the three wells of Minster, and at the first, the Well of the Triple Goddess, he discovered 'an image that may date back to pre-Celtic times'. According to rumour this image was handled by an archaeologist whose wife had struggled to conceive a child resulting in several miscarriages; nine months later, however, she gave birth to a beautiful daughter. Eason adds that, 'Five other "miracle" babies have been born to parents who were experiencing fertility or pregnancy difficulties and who have handled the image.'

In the second well an emblem representing Diana Triformis was unearthed. Diana was known as the triple goddess, represented by a young woman (maiden), a birth-giving matron (mother) and an elderly woman (crone). These three variants were said to represent three differing phases of the moon with the maiden signifying the new moon, the matron characterising the full moon and the crone as a sign of the waning moon.

In the third well a bronze ritual object was discovered, and was believed to have given the waters of the well curative properties.

'But what has all of this got to do with the woman in white?' I hear you ask.

Well, in 1996 Mr Slade had a peculiar encounter whilst sitting up in bed. Mr Slade's home at the time was situated close to the ley line, and he had been pondering a summary he had written for a book in regards to an ancient Celtic goddess when his attention was suddenly drawn to a woman standing at the foot of his bed. The figure was glowing in white, dressed in white robes and yet vanished before his eyes. He recalled, 'I have seen the White Lady before several times out of the corner of my eye and beyond the field of vision, an indistinct shape beyond my bedroom door.'

Brian wondered if his archaeological forays at the wells had somehow triggered this motherly goddess. However, whilst some could argue that maybe, just maybe, Brian was actually asleep and dreaming, there are others who've seen the woman in white in the area. Those who have observed the woman describe her as 'like a bride on her wedding day' who always disappears when witnesses approach her. According to Cassandra Eason others have experienced 'a strong scent of flowers or perfume' whilst some witnesses have even seen the woman in white hovering over the fertility image as if she is some sort of guardian. It seems, however, that the excavations of the wells have done more than simply uncover one spirit. The well known as Abbess' Well, which sits close by to the Triple Goddess Well, has also been known to have medicinal powers. It now sits in someone's back garden, but those who once wished to see it could book an appointment. The well may be named after a nun of superiority who was transferred from Newington to Sheppey. No one is quite sure how this nun died but some believe that her body was found down in the well.

It's no surprise that the house which harbours the well is reputedly haunted. Items have flown off walls of their own accord in the past, whilst ghostly footsteps have also been heard. Psychic mediums who have visited the premises claim to have seen nuns within the vicinity, walking around the well. One witness to a ghostly nun was of the opinion that the reason the apparition had appeared was simply due to the fact that it wasn't happy with the water from the well having been scooped up and stored in an old whiskey bottle.

It's no real surprise either that ghostly monks have also been seen around Minster. One such figure has been seen to be reading a book whilst resting under a tree near the church. According to Eason, 'Two monks were said to officiate at Minster in the reign of Henry I, one as curate and one as confessor to the nuns.' This brings us to another ghostly episode which took place in the 1950s and involved a young girl named Barbara Woods. She had visited the abbey and seen phantom monks

which she recorded in the visitor's book. Many years later as a young, engaged woman, Barbara revisited the abbey with her fiancé and was given a guided tour by Brian Slade. Barbara's partner mentioned to Brian that Miss Woods had seen monks quite regularly, to which Mr Slade replied that there had been no monks in the area in her lifetime. Barbara was adamant that as a child she'd seen the monks assembled near a gate leading to the garden area of Minster Vicarage. Brian added, '… this is interesting, because the small door leading into the oldest part of the abbey church and known as the priests' or monks' door, is right alongside the garden gate'.

As with the case of many alleged spirits, many sightings are down to interpretation and possibly moulded

Minster Abbey church – the haunt of phantom monks.

Rear view of the Gatehouse Museum.

by the belief system that the witness holds. For instance, as Cassandra Eason adds in regards to the ghostly woman in white, 'It does add some weight to the argument made previously that ley lines provide a psychic energy which is shaped to the viewers' expectations, so that Christians see the White Lady as the Virgin Mary while pagans view her as a White Goddess.' And there are those of course who simply see the spectre as a nun, or more prosaically as just a ghostly woman in white. Even so, witnesses are clearly seeing something around the gatehouse but that's not where the mystery ends. Brian Slade had another unusual episode whilst waiting to take a photograph of the third well, situated at what was Minster Garden Centre. A skull had been unearthed and Brian placed the object on a set of steps in order to

photograph it but his expensive camera failed to work on every occasion – and yet every other item Brian had captured had come out just fine. Eventually the skull was interred at its original resting place. It seems though that the reputed spectres of the gatehouse are in fact guardians, of a sort. In 1974 a Mrs Sylvia Brooke visited the abbey gatehouse with her small dog, but as she was about to enter the building her pet pulled her away, as if sensing something wasn't right. Sylvia attempted once again to enter the building but again her dog wrenched her away. Seconds later an old drainpipe dislodged from the wall, bringing down rubble, moss and bird faeces on the exact spot where Sylvia had been standing but moved away, thanks to her dog. Had the dog sensed this imminent disaster or were there unseen spirits at work?

Is it also possible that one or even a few of the spirits said to haunt the nearby site of old Sheppey General Hospital are also connected to the ley line theory? Although the hospital was demolished decades ago and replaced by flats, when it was an infirmary a woman in pale attire was once thought to roam the Upper B section, known as the De Shurland ward. Nurses who observed the wraith claimed that the figure drifted from bed to bed as if searching for someone, but no one found out who the ghost could have been. The hospital had been built on ground that was once occupied by an old workhouse that burnt down. According to Sheila M. Judge, one particular nurse whilst on night duty in the maternity unit had a peculiar encounter. The nurse had heard footsteps in the below corridor, suggesting that a patient or member of staff was about to enter the unit – and this was confirmed when she heard the resounding click of the door, but when she found nobody present she called the night security, believing that the hospital may have had an intruder. Bizarrely, the same episode was experienced on two further occasions by the nurse, and the final time she boldly rushed to the doors, throwing them open, only to be greeted by the silence of an empty corridor. After this eerie night, every time the footsteps were heard, the nurse chose to ignore them until one evening, when she felt a firm hand upon her shoulder. Although startled, the nurse turned around to face the person, only to find no one in sight. Some believe the ghostly figure is one Helena Winter, a nurse who worked at the Sheppey Workhouse Infirmary. She died in 1893 of an infection after treating a seriously ill patient.

There's no doubt that hospitals – especially at night, when all is rather quiet – can be rather eerie places. Whether it's the long, cold corridors or the deserted basement areas, they are the sort of places where the mind can run wild. A chap named Kevin who used to work at the hospital also experienced the reputed spirits. He worked for the hospital radio station, but one night whilst walking along a corridor away from the X-ray wing he felt a strong compulsion to turn around. When he did he saw a fleeting figure, dressed in black, rush across the passage. Kevin wasn't frightened of the spectre and began to enquire about it to local staff who told him that he may have seen the phantom nun. On another occasion, again while working at night, Kevin noted how whilst in the radio studio, vinyl records began to fly off the shelves of their own accord.

When I write about sites of old hospitals etc., people tend to ask as to whether anyone has experienced anything paranormal whilst living in or visiting newer buildings erected on these sites. Well, the answer to that is yes. I was told that the houses which now sit on the site of the old hospital have been plagued by weird occurrences. On one occasion, quite recently, a homeowner became rather spooked when they found that their fridge had been completely turned around in the kitchen. The person in question had gone out to work and upon returning home found the fridge facing the opposite way! In another building a young boy told his parents that in the night someone had entered his room and tickled his feet. The parents were rather spooked by this as they recalled hearing their son giggling in the night, but passed it off as a dream.

Haunted Houses

In May 2013 I was telephoned by a woman who told me of an incredible series of events that had plagued her and her family over the last few years. Originally from London, the woman in question had moved to Sheppey in 2006 to a house that was built in the 1990s. Although the area is off the beaten track, so to say, she didn't expect to have to call in three sets of people to exorcise the house. It began just after she moved in, with strange sounds; her daughter reported that one night as she slept upstairs she could hear the sound of someone dragging a chain outside her window. However, most of the activity seemed to involve any pets the woman may have had, especially dogs. She told me:

> It's as if the house or whatever haunts it doesn't like animals – I've had several dogs, both small and large, and they've either vanished or been so spooked they've literally run away. Apart from the strange occurrences with the dogs the activity doesn't really bother me, I laugh at it, but I've had the house up for sale on two occasions and no one takes an interest, it's as if whatever is here wants me to stay here.

Several ghost hunters and mediums were called to the house and each had differing opinions on what exactly was plaguing the property. The woman added:

> The first person to come and investigate the house said that an old woman was around, whilst the second group sensed a ghost in the bedroom. The third lot of people to visit the house said that the ghosts want to keep me here because I remind them of a family member, but I've also been told that ghostly animals lurk here, pigs, cats – and that maybe it used to be a farm or a slaughterhouse. Stranger still, I was told that the house sits on a pathway which acts as some type of portal for spirits and other shape-shifters.

One particular haunted house has become embedded into Sheppey folklore. Tams cottages were said to have been built by a ship's carpenter many years ago. Initially the man was not welcome on the island, as he had been part of the Dutch convoy that had visited England on one of their hostile expeditions. The Dutchman was left behind, but eventually became accepted by the islanders due to his construction skills. Tams cottages were a pair, one of which he occupied, renting out the other. However, after finally becoming settled on Sheppey, the carpenter became involved in a love triangle after meeting a local maiden. Tragically for the carpenter, the maiden was also being lusted after by a local man, and although the woman refused his advances, the islander took out his fury on the Dutchman and shortly afterwards the carpenter seemed to mysteriously vanish without trace. Although no one knew what exactly had happened to the carpenter, rumour was rife that he'd been murdered and so his ghost was said to stalk the premises of Tams cottages.

Nowadays the cottages have been converted into one but whether the ghost of the carpenter is happy with this alteration, we'll just have to wait and see!

Several years ago a chap named Tim Wood visited a fourteenth-century house at Oak Lane which belonged to a friend of his. He had been accompanied by a few friends when they entered the old house, with Tim being the last to cross the threshold. However, upon entering he recalled how 'I suddenly felt extremely cold even though the temperature outside was in the eighties'. When Tim mentioned this to his colleagues he was met with derision; after all, his friends were sweating due to the blistering heat. However, the chap who owned the house asked if Tim was feeling okay, to which Tim then asked if there used to be a staircase by the front door. The house owner gave Tim a quizzical look and enquired, 'Are you psychic?' to which Tim replied in the negative.

'Well,' replied Tim's friend, 'there did indeed used to be a staircase by the door, but that was a century ago,' to which Tim responded, 'There's something really weird about your house. I can't stay in here, I'm really freezing.'

The fellow who owned the property immediately returned that the house most certainly had a supernatural presence, adding, 'The dog won't stay downstairs at night and we find things have been moved around.'

Before he left the house Tim rather sceptically suggested that maybe the man's children had been responsible for moving the household items around but this was met with dismissal: 'My wife has actually seen it … she was sitting in bed one night reading when she looked up and saw a little old lady sitting on the bottom of the bed wearing a smocked top and a poke bonnet.' According to the man's wife the ghostly old woman kept muttering words to the effect of 'Oh dear! Oh dear!' and then disappeared the moment Tim's friend entered the bedroom. Tim was rather perturbed by his experience at the house, and recalled that 'I told my friend that I wouldn't be visiting him again!'

Another haunted house was once situated at Scocles Road in Minster. Over a decade ago, a chap who resided at the house decided to take a holiday abroad but decided that before leaving, as a safety precaution he would rig up a recording advice that would pick up any noises should anyone attempt to break into the property. When the man returned from his break and played the tape back he heard the usual sounds of the postman popping letters through the door but was then rather surprised to hear what sounded like monks chanting. A few days later the man decided to play the tape to his friends and asked them what they thought of the noises; they all agreed that it sounded like some type of chanting. Could such monks have been the same spirits often said to have frequented Minster Abbey in life and in death? When one considers that the abbey is a short distance from Scocles Road, it would be no surprise.

A Haunted Pub and More …

Many years ago it was reputed that the Prince of Waterloo public house – situated on Minster Road but now no longer in business – was haunted by a phantom nun. The ghostly woman was said to have been named Agatha who, unlike so many rumoured spooks, was far from being the troublesome spirit many would expect. In fact, the local customers of the pub had become so used to Agatha that on occasion it was said that the spectre was even known to sit down for a pint of Guinness or two – which gives a whole new meaning to the term spirits on tap! According to the *Gazette & Times*,

The Prince of Waterloo pub was said to be haunted by a female spirit named Agatha.

Agatha was only mischievous at times, with the paper stating:

Doors were violently slammed or mysteriously opened and the lights flickered on and off. Family pets were not keen on going anywhere near the cellar and people had cold sensations while working on the books in the kitchen. Agatha's favourite tricks with the pumps were on Friday nights when the pub was at its busiest. Sometimes the gas was turned off in the cellar five or six times a night, often so tightly it took a wrench to get the gas back on. One former customer reported seeing a glass flying off the bar in the pub – unaided by human hand. An empty bottle of Guinness was sometimes found in the middle of the cellar – although the cellar was always locked.

The main legend concerning Agatha, however, was that she often appeared to guard a secret tunnel that ran beneath the public house. No one really knows what treasures – or horrors – lurk within that hidden tunnel but several psychic investigators have in the past warned that should anyone attempt to knock down the wall and enter the tunnel, then they shall suffer a terrible fate. Just behind the pub can be found what is known as Dancing Dolly Hill. This small alleyway has long been the haunted of a non-descript, shadowy figure – maybe the victim of one of those hangings said to have taken place many years ago. Rumour has it that the walkway got its morbid name due to the fact that bodies which were hung from gibbets would often twitch and spasm in the throes

Former site of the Prince of Waterloo pub.

of death and then dangle limply, like ghastly dolls. However, there is a less macabre theory as to the name of the walkway; many years ago, according to historian Brian Slade, '... naval ratings were marched up there every Sunday to attend church parade at Minster Abbey. Tradition tells how the local lassies used to line the route, jumping excitedly, waving and making eyes at the sailors ...'

Another pub, situated not too far from the Prince of Waterloo is the King's Arms. This pub is also said to be haunted by a ghostly nun. Although sightings seem scarce, the phantom makes itself known due to the tip-toe of its steps descending the stairs of the cellar. Whether such pubs are really haunted is open to debate, but a majority of inns do seem to harbour spooks – and maybe this is

simply to attract the customers who, with ale in hand, can sit around a flickering log fire at Christmas and discuss such alleged ghouls. However, in most cases concerning reputedly haunted pubs, it is often said that the resident ghost is responsible for the flickering lights, the cold spot in the corner of the room, the creak on the stair and the swaying tankards that hang off the beams. After all, you've got to blame someone! The Elm Tree pub on the Lower Road, Minster, has been closed for a short while but it hasn't stopped the rumours of a ghostly presence. The entities present could well be some of the soldiers who stopped by this inn during the First World War – the premises might have been one of the last places the troops felt happiest before going into battle. It's no surprise that the occasional ghost hunt has taken place within the inn. One such event took place in the summer of 2013 and the usual creaks and bangs, often associated with old derelict buildings, were reported. The investigators on hand attempted to contact any resident spirits and claimed to have reached a young boy named Timmy who was accompanied by fluctuations in temperature and the often-debated EVP (Electronic Voice Phenomena), where investigators often ask questions into the atmosphere and record their questions in the hope of capturing any spectral answers on tape. As expected in such an investigation, the psychic mediums claimed to have picked up and observed a number of spirits but could not verify this to others present. Sceptics in such an atmosphere would no doubt dismiss such 'experiences' as the power of the mind and in a number of cases in regards to reputedly haunted buildings, evidence is often lacking. Whilst some people present at such venues claim to see spirits there are others who cannot, whilst in other cases seemingly odd noises or atmospherics may be witnessed by some and not others. Does this suggest that certain people are more sensitive to certain 'entities' or that such alleged spirits are merely a product of the human psyche connected to a certain individual?

In 2013 I was contacted by a lady named Teresa who told me of a brief, albeit strange ghostly encounter which involved her sister-in-law who, as a child, whilst walking in fields with friends at the back of Harps Avenue had observed a pair of boots which were walking through the mist. The boots – which were black and sported a large buckle – were certainly strange, as they appeared to not be connected to any body!

One Sheppey legend which has always fascinated me concerns some of the alleged tunnels said to wind their way beneath some of the old buildings and churches of the island. Such passageways have had many uses over the years with some of the opinion that they were the hiding place for smugglers eager to conceal their contraband, whilst there are those who claim that nuns would use such tunnels as an escape should they sense danger. Tunnels, just like dusty attics and damp basements, tend to be the ideal setting for a ghost story or two – maybe it's the claustrophobic atmosphere, the overwhelming darkness or the whole clandestine nature of such passageways but either way, not many people have been brave enough to explore these dark realms. However, a few years ago it was said that a tunnel at Minster was explored by a local man. One afternoon he set off into the gloom, armed with an old sword, only to return as white as a ghost and unable to mutter a single word about what horrors he had seen. Strangely though, despite the intrigue of this story, this is very similar to the tale of the brave fiddler who descended into one of the tunnels rumoured to exist below the ancient priory at Aylesford, near Maidstone. However, on this occasion the fiddler, who told those in attendance that he would set off into the darkness all the while playing his fiddle – never returned, but this is in fact a popular urban legend, and one which has surfaced through Britain. For instance, there is a similar tale attached to the Devil's Hole in Hertfordshire, once frequented by a local man named Blind George, who told locals that as he had no fear of darkness he would, armed with a fiddle, venture into the blackness, the sound of his playing being the only sign of his whereabouts. He too perished, only this time emerging from the tunnel consumed by fire. They make for great stories, but are they true? You decide.

Another ghostly tale from the island concerns an area known as the Lower Wards in Minster. An old farm that used to sit in the Lower Ward had various stables and one of these was believed to have been haunted by a spectral horse, although the family that resided had no clue as to why. No one ever saw the phantom animal but some laid claim to having actually heard the beast snorting and rattling its headgear. Sadly the area in question has since been replaced by houses. The story of the phantom horse is covered in the 8 September 1977 issue of the *Sheppey Gazette* under the headline, 'The ghostly horse down on the farm' with Sheila M. Judge being quoted as saying that the spectral creature is probably a remnant of a collection of animals once kept at the farm. The paper, in reference to Sheila's experiences on the farm adds, 'She [Sheila] tells of the time a visitor to the farm, who was warned about the ghost horse, and said he did not believe in ghosts,' could be seen 'at the dead of night wandering about the farmyard looking for a non-existent horse that kept making strange noises and interrupting his sleep.'

The Girl Who Came Back to Life ...

One story that most certainly deserves attention, even though it sounds like something out of a film, is mentioned in Minster folklore and dates back several centuries to the late 1400s. It is stated that a 1-year-old girl called Ann, the child of a Thomas Plott who lived in a cottage in the town, was run over by a dung cart as she played along a main road. A farmhand who worked for the nuns was too slow to react upon seeing the girl and the heavy wheel of his cart crushed the poor child. According to reports from the time the cart had wheels reinforced with iron plates and so the child was pinned to the ground by the monstrosity, her body left as 'flat as a pancake'. Many locals flocked to the scene of the accident only to find the child dead and the commotion roused Ann's mother, who emerged from her house and ran to the aid of her child, but it was too late. As she embraced Ann's crumpled, lifeless body, she could only scream in anger before returning her daughter to the ground and chasing after the driver of the cart, blaring at him in fury. However, the incident had come to the attention of another local woman who, according to reports 'was firmly established in the Grace of Christ'. The woman took a purse from her garment, approached the dead girl and according to historian Sheila M. Judge, 'bent a penny over the lifeless corpse, as if to implore the pity of our Lord and the prayers of his most devout servant King Henry by this promise of an offering'. Those who stood by prayed and prayed hard when suddenly the little girl cried out, and pleaded for her mother – even stranger was the fact that the girl had never previously spoken before. Weirder still, within a few hours the girl was back to her normal self, somehow restored by this marvellous miracle bestowed upon her.

As the story is rather old we'll never really know its truth, but there is every suggestion that little Ann came back from the dead as part of a seemingly supernatural act.

Phantom Smells ...

Ghosts really do seem to make themselves known in all manner of ways. Under the heading of 'What! Another ghost story?' the *Sheerness Times Guardian* of 8 December 1961 reports that 'The succulent aroma of fried steak and onions fills the bar at Minster Working Men's Club three times a week, completely baffling members by its regularity.' According to the article the club sits on a site 'once occupied by a convent, a stone's throw from Minster Abbey church'.

Club secretary Mr Sid Corthorne reported that, 'We can only suggest that the nuns choose to do their cooking just before our closing time. Who else could it be?'

The delightful aroma was first noted by Mr Corthorne's wife and at first he scoffed at such an idea until he experienced the spectral waft. He added, 'Our members don't mind. They regard the smell as a pleasant warning that they have only about five minutes in which to buy their last drink and go home!'

Minster Working Men's Club, haunted by a phantom smell!

3

QUIRKY QUEENBOROUGH

Queenborough was, according to historian John Maruis Wilson, 'a village and parish' in Sheppey that 'superseded a Saxon place Cyningburg or King's-Castle where annual courts were held; was founded, along with a castle, by Edward III, and called Queenborough in compliment to his queen Philippa …'

In 1382 the castle suffered damage to two of its towers when an earthquake struck. In 1648, according to the Queenborough Harbour's website, the castle was 'surveyed and condemned – it was sold for demolition two years later and Queenborough lost its most notable landmark'. A well which once belonged to the castle was said to harbour curative powers – the water was said to be medicinal, unlike the 'unwholesome and brackish water elsewhere in the town'. Smuggling was once said to be rife within the parish with the criminals operating in some of the cellars beneath houses. In January 1981 human remains, believed to be victims of cholera, were discovered at a local creek.

Queerness at a Queenborough House …

In 2013 I was contacted by a lady named Alice Bodiam who relayed to me an intriguing history of personal experiences concerning her house in Queenborough High Street. She commented:

In the 1900s a man called Edward Kemp brought our house and built an undertakers on the land behind it. A man called Jess Bentley worked at the undertakers and also rented out our house from Edward with his wife Bess Bentley. My uncle also used to work at the under takers when he was a teenager. Since the age of twelve I started hearing things and seeing shadows out of the corner of my eye. I saw orbs bouncing down the hallways, heard people calling my name, the feeling of people watching me; the simple little things. It gradually got more and more; I would hear footsteps running up and down the stairs and then I started to see spirits. Spirits don't scare me, but there's one experience I'll never forget and it's the last day I ever saw a spirit. But I'll keep that one for last.

The very first thing I heard was someone whispering 'kishan' over and over again. I've always been curious as to what that means, to me it sounded like a name. The very first spirit I saw was quite strange and to be fair I still don't know if it was real or whether I was day-dreaming. I was sleeping and I don't know why I did but I woke up, I turned over to my side and just saw a head above my wardrobe. Strange I know, and I'm still unsure about that one because it looked a bit like my dad. On another occasion I was sitting on my bunk-bed at the time – on the top bunk reading a book. I remember feeling a tug on my hair and general poking. A few minutes after, out of the corner of my eye I saw a white lady figure running towards the ladders on the bed. I remember she wore a white flowing gown or nighty and short curly hair. With every spirit I've experienced I've never seen their face – only ever the indents of their eyes and their nose whilst their whole face is shaded in one colour. I've seen the woman a couple more times roaming around the house.

I've seen a lot of ghostly animals. Like cats running under chairs or running past you but there's nothing there. The most vivid animal I ever saw was an old dog of ours called Jessica; she was a cocker spaniel. I was in our dining room and I saw what I thought to be our dog at the time, Charlie, sitting at our backdoor, but as I called her to come closer I saw to my left my sister was standing there with our dog. Looking back at the back door she was gone. The image was so clear it was unreal. However, now we come to Jess Bentley. My family smell his cigarette smoke from time to time but no one has seen him, except me. Like I said, I'll never forget this day. It was late and me, my mum and my sister were in our kitchen talking, my mum handed me a couple of black bin bags and asked me to take the bins out, it was quite dark outside but not pitch black. I opened our back door and walked out but was forced to stop by a man which I believed to be Jess Bentley. As I looked up I saw this very tall, skinny man. He was all in black, even his face, and he was wearing a top hat, a t-shirt tucked into smart trousers, pointed black shoes and a cloak with red lining. He had a very big pointed nose. He was clear as day and I saw everything. It was such a surprise to the point I chucked the bags and went to run inside but tripped and fell in the door. He is the closest I've ever come to a spirit, and unfortunately this was the last time I ever saw anything. His gravestone is at the top of my road at Queenborough High Street. I've never seen what he looks like in pictures; it would be nice to see if the man I saw was in fact Jess.

All of this happened in the space of three years between the ages of twelve and fifteen. After seeing Jess the only thing that happened was hearing voices and seeing the odd animal spirit here and there. I was awoken from my sleep by a very deep man's voice calling my name, it was very close, I responded to him while I was half asleep, half-awake but didn't hear nothing back. I've only ever seen spirits or had things happen to me while at my house, nothing has ever happened outside of my house.

I was fascinated by Alice's experiences and enquired as to whether other family members had seen or felt anything unusual. Alice replied:

> It's not only me that's experienced things in our house. When my twin sister Emily was about twelve she was awoken in the night by the appearance of a short man; quite big (round) and dressed in a suit and wearing a hat. He had a moustache and was standing at our bedroom door accompanied by a Jack Russell dog. My dad has also had a few encounters. He's had items such as plants pulled down next to him as well as being poked hard in the arms, and having his name called. One night while he was sleeping he had the feeling of a cat walking over him, the covers moved down just like it would when a cat walks.

Alice concluded that, 'Our house is very old and has so much character and I'm sure I've still got a lot to experience and see. I hope my stories are helpful.'

Spooky Snippets

Strangely, ghost stories from Queenborough seem rather few and far between but I guess it's all a matter of who you speak to. One such brief tale which springs to mind concerns a pet shop which sat in the vicinity of what is known as Nellie's Alley in the town. A woman who used to live above the pet shop mentioned that her residence had been the haunt of three ghosts – a man and two children – but no one seems sure as to who these spirits are.

In 2007 a ghost investigation was conducted at an undisclosed property in Queenborough after the owner claimed experiencing supernatural activity in certain rooms. Five people were in attendance at the twentieth-century property, including the owner, but the investigative team of four made their way to different rooms of the house to see if they could pick up anything unusual. The first spirit to be picked up was that of an elderly female who told one team member that she had passed in the house, but most of the activity seemed to take place in the children's bedroom. The main spirit said to have been detected was that of an old man who may have possibly died in battle. Sadly, such 'contact' is rarely verified and it has often been argued that certain spirit presences are more likely connected to the medium in general rather than the building. Lack of evidence in such investigations obviously leaves such research open to debate.

In October 2013 I spoke to a Sheerness lady who stated that as a child she was often warned away from a certain spot near Queenborough because it was meant to be haunted. The spot, not far from Whiteway Road in the town, was rumoured to be the haunt of a young woman. Children were often spooked by an alleyway in the area and believe the ghost to be that of Eliza Coppins who, in 1857, was murdered by a man named Prentis. Some records state that the woman was killed in a 'crime of passion' in the vicinity of Pier Cottages, since demolished, but those who recall the eerie legend maintain that the area in question slightly differs to details in print. In 2013 island resident Paul Deadman told me of a haunted building at Queenborough.

He stated that in the past 'footsteps were regularly heard at the building off of Whiteway Road. I think it used to be called Wasso's or something similar; it's now Swale Building Supplies but I'm not sure whether it's the same building.'

In 1975 a Reg Witts occupied the Town House in Queenborough High Street. The building adjoined what became known as the Guildhall Museum – a late eighteenth-century property which was erected on the site of the original Market House and had been captured during the Dutch invasion of 1667. The building boasts a small prison, but when I spoke to a member of staff in 2013 I was rather surprised to hear that no ghostly tales had been reported. However, when Mr Witts and his wife Sylvia resided in the Town House, there was enough weird and wonderful activity to almost scare the couple out of their – excuse the pun – wits! Reg was not prone to flights of fancy and had been a hardened seaman, so when he moved into the Town House in 1972 along with his wife and two daughters he didn't expect to encounter any ghostly shenanigans. Reg had only lived in the house permanently since 1975 due to work commitments, and despite being an islander, commented, 'When I settled in Queenborough, ghosts were the last thing I considered.'

According to a press report from March 1975 the house is described thus: 'Even in daylight it's spooky, but night-time's flitting shadows can be unnerving.' The main ghost of the

The Guildhall Museum at Queenborough, situated next to a pair of reputedly haunted houses.

building is described as a '… lady of easy virtue who met her end at the hands of a butcher … her body is supposed to have been found in the alleyway alongside the Town House, but perhaps it is the tale of the sea captain without a ship who continues to walk the bridge (in other words, the top landing) which has most significance.' The spectre is said to wander aimlessly, dragging his feet. Such is the weight of the weary sea captain that from downstairs one can see the floorboards creaking and the ceiling lights swaying.

Mr Witts reported, 'I was prepared to dismiss the stories as rubbish, but after working on the house for a year I've mixed feelings. Admittedly, it makes me feel stupid, but on one occasion not so long ago, I was so terrified I locked myself in a room.'

But what sort of horror could cause an ex-merchant seaman to become afraid of his own house?

Mr Witts was quick to add, 'I was alone in the house fixing ceiling tiles when suddenly I saw a dark shape loom across the landing followed by a definite creaking of floor boards. I was so scared I scrambled down the steps, locked myself in the library and kept my back to the door.' Despite fleeing in terror from the supposed spirits Reg certainly felt no animosity towards them, stating, 'Neither of us feel there is anything sinister about the place but there is a definite atmosphere', to the extent that Reg's daughters, Kerry and Kyra, had to sleep in their rooms with the light on.

When Reg had his creepy encounter he was rather embarrassed to tell his wife but when he finally plucked up the

Town House (left) with Town Villa on the right – both supposedly haunted houses.

The River Swale, haunt of a spectral vessel and its rugged sea captain.

courage to speak to her she responded, 'I've been terrified by shadows in the breakfast room, and strange noises on the top landing.'

The huge house was said to have boasted some eleven bedrooms and to have been built as the local mayor's residence, and because of its history the Witts were keen to stay, with Reg adding, 'It is a beautiful old house with plenty of space to move around in. It would take more than a ghost to frighten us away.'

When Reg began working on the building he was adamant that the house would have to keep its character, with only the door to the Guildhall being bricked up. Whether such renovations caused the ghostly activity we will never really know, but Reg concluded that, 'Even if we had a dozen ghosts [in] clanking armour, a few headless horsemen and knights we wouldn't want to move – we love it here.'

Interestingly, when I visited Queenborough in the autumn of 2013 I bumped into a chap who was washing his car just a few yards from the Town House.

I told him that I was writing a book on local ghosts and he commented:

There was once said to be a ghost of a little girl in the Town Villa which sits next to the Town House. It was rumoured that the girl   dressed in old-fashioned clothing – haunted the top floor where there used to be a salon, and customers would often comment about the pretty little girl on the stairs but upon investigation staff could find no one. She really spooked a few people that I knew but I don't know if people still see her now that it's a house.

Returning back to the alleged sea captain spectre of the Town House, it's also worth noting that the River Swale is sometimes said to be haunted by a phantom vessel. Could it be the same boat which ran aground in a creek near Oare – a small village on the other side of the Swale – known for its haunted pub, The Shipwright's Arms which just happens to be haunted by a sea captain?

4

SUPERNATURAL LEYSDOWN

The town of Leysdown, also referred to as Leysdown-on-Sea, gets its name from the Saxon 'leswe' meaning pasture, and 'dun' denoting hill. In Domesday Book Leysdown is referred to as Legesdun. The town is known for its amusements and arcades. In 1750 the remains of an elephant jutting out of the clay were discovered by a Mr Jacob.

Leysdown's coastal waters are said to be haunted by a ghostly fisherman.

The Phantom Fisherman

Chronicler Charles Igglesden wrote of an interesting haunting at Leysdown stating that at one point a famous fisherman, who was fishing with nets off Leysdown – during a time when it was prohibited to do so – was caught by a bailiff. In panic he shot his captor but to avoid being executed for his crime he jumped into his boat and fled. However, once out at sea off Leysdown, he jumped into the foaming waters and drowned. It is said that on the anniversary of his death the phantom fisherman appears, from the shoulders up, in the water.

Those fortunate (or should I say unfortunate?) enough to have seen the spectre remark that he is snagged in a fishing net. Sadly no date is given for the suicide, meaning that those who hope to see the ghost could be waiting a long time on the beach. Igglesden concludes his tale, saying that 'no one ever saw the ghost but other believers argued that the spook only appeared when the wind was at a certain spot'.

Leysdown seems rather reticent to give up any of its ghostly history, if it has any to offer. This is no surprise when one discovers that the area isn't much more than a few holiday homes and marshland.

5

WEIRDNESS AT WARDEN BAY

Warden (often referred to as Warden Bay) can be found situated next to Leysdown-on-Sea. It is a small holiday village facing the sea. At the point where the cliffs are inaccessible it is known as Warden Point.

Warden Manor

Warden Manor is a delightfully old building dating back to the sixteenth century (although a story which appeared in the *Times Guardian* of 14 July 1972 stated that the manor 'dates back to the tenth century' whilst another report in the *Times Guardian* of 22 July 1977 states 'thirteenth century'!) which, during the Second World War, became a convalescent home and then afterwards a monastery which housed more than fifty monks. Over the years many buildings have fallen into the sea off Warden Bay due to cliff erosion but thankfully Warden Manor still stands. The manor was once part of Warden Court and according to the Sheppey Website was 'given to Sir Thomas Cheyne by King Henry VIII'.

It was once believed that beneath the manor wind several tunnels which would have possibly, if rumours are believed, wormed their way to Shurland Hall or a local public house, although this hasn't been verified. Centuries ago the shorelines of Sheppey would have been used by smugglers and so these tunnels may have acted as ideal places to conceal contraband, and such passageways may have provided ideal escape routes for a criminal or two. It's no real surprise that Warden Manor is said to be haunted by a number of spooks, including a woman dressed in old-fashioned attire. Mysterious figures, possibly those of smugglers, were also once rumoured to haunt the area, although smugglers were often known to invent ghostly tales in order to keep prying eyes away from their illegal stash. The main spectre said to haunt the manor is that of one John Sawbridge, who, a few centuries previous resided there and who was believed to have led a smuggling gang. The spectre of Mr Sawbridge would make quite an arresting sight, for it is said to appear on

Warden Manor – one of Sheppey's oldest houses.

horseback galloping through the trees on blustery nights. Sawbridge, although never allegedly apprehended for his crimes, was said to have died after taking a fall from his horse one night. He wasn't found until the next day, by which time his injuries had worsened resulting in his death the following day.

On 9 September 2012 Chrissie Daniels, writing for *Kent News*, reported that Warden Manor was up for sale. Former owners Mr Fred Lardeaux, and his wife Vivienne knew all about the resident spectre. According to a snippet from the *Gazette & Times* from the late 1980s, Mr Lardeaux had sat up one night hoping to spot the ghost, but sadly dropped off. The couple never did see the reputed spectre, according to sources, despite having a number of less notable experiences, including strange voices and smells.

Mind you, that *Times Guardian* article from 22 July 1977 does mention that Fred did have an encounter with 'his ghostly namesake "Fred the Savage"', although there are no details of this experience. The article goes on to mention another ghost at the manor however – that of a woman named Jenny, 'wife of Delamark Banks'; she is said to prowl the nursery on dark nights. The report concludes that 'Jenny (known to some as Sawbridge) lost a child at birth and died shortly afterwards. Still she returns to mourn her grief.'

There could be a number of ghosts, mounted on equally spectral horses, rumoured to haunt the Sheppey cliffs. Some of these shades could be the ghosts of revenue officers who plummeted to their deaths over the cliffs whilst on horseback in pursuit of those elusive smugglers who had hidden in

The rear of Warden Manor.

Warden Manor is full of passageways, hidden rooms and secret tunnels.

nearby thickets. It is possible that due to the overwhelming darkness on certain nights, the pursuers – whilst charging through the wilds atop the cliffs – did not see the sudden drop just yards ahead. By the time they did it was too late and they fell to their deaths. It is said that even over the last few years people have heard the sound of horses' hooves galloping around outside Warden Manor and yet no animal or rider has revealed itself in the flesh. Some claim that the spectral horse is one of the island's most reliable spirits, in that it makes itself known on 18 December every year.

More recently it was recorded that a man working in the manor had a frightening experience when he observed a ghostly old woman dressed in old-fashioned attire that drifted across the room and disappeared through a wall.

The frightened witness was rather hesitant to speak of his episode but one day plucked up the courage to tell the caretaker of the building. The caretaker wasn't too surprised and replied that he'd become rather accustomed to hearing so many ghostly tales attached to the house.

During a crisp autumnal day I visited Warden Manor with my wife. We were welcomed by the new owners, Elsie and Brian, who had taken on the empty, rather dilapidated manor as a project and were hoping to restore it to its former glory and eventually live there. It was an absolute privilege to be shown inside, around all those dusty nooks and crannies and empty rooms. The manor is an absolute joy to behold; even through the cobwebs, every secret door and dark corner seemed to ooze history. I asked the couple just how

Some of the unusual poster-like artwork on the old walls of Warden Manor.

Old fireplace at the manor. The floorboards in front of it could well hide a secret tunnel.

old the manor really is and they replied, 'Records seem to date back to about 1540 but it's probably older than that – over the years it has been used as a holiday camp which was run by a charitable trust called Toc H as well as a small hospital and convalescent home.'

We were shown the boarded floor said to hide secret subterranean passageways and also experienced a wealth of rooms where soldiers were once stationed during the wars. There were even plaques on the walls to signify where certain people had stayed, including someone identified only as the 'Unknown Warrior'. In the past some of these rooms were given themes and had a variety of names such as Zebra, The Ark, Elephant, Lion, The Orient Express and Little Orient. Some of the wallpaper had been stripped from some of the rooms, revealing intriguing poster-like designs. In the past it was said that a rhyme had been written on one of the walls, reading, 'Here we serve the Warden hags, casting spells in paper bags; Curse on you witches all, who made poor Vic drive through the wall.'

This verse, accompanied by a sketch of a witch on a broomstick, would have been in reference to former manor owner Vic Martin, who had pranged his vehicle.

Upstairs we marvelled at the many small rooms and the adjoining outbuilding erected by the monks who had left just years before, along with several holy garden remnants. Brian told me, 'One of the monks named Mario was a caretaker to the building when the Order had left, and he spoke of strange things happening in the house.'

I was keen to find out more about the reputed ghosts, and the couple continued:

We've heard of the stories, and just a few decades ago a cleaner was said to have fallen down a shaft in the manor and died and some claim they have seen her. Mario [the monk] told us that 'if you ever see the ghostly woman, don't be afraid of her …' but we've never really seen anything. Maybe because we are applying some tender loving care to the building the alleged ghosts are happy!

However, after walking through the labyrinth Elsie did mention that on one occasion she had been inside the house filming with her camcorder, when she heard a deep male voice say something in an indecipherable language. When one considers just how many different people have stayed in and visited the manor, it's no wonder that such a glorious building holds so much energy.

My wife and I eventually left Elsie and Brian to their project and wished them well, although I did tell them to keep me up to date should anything spooky happen.

Haunted Hotel

Warden Bay Hotel, situated on Jetty Road, was once believed to be haunted. A Mr Paine, writing on the Voices of Leysdown website, commented that in the 1950s his sister-in-law had worked at the coffee shop stationed within the hotel. She told Mr Paine that the hotel was meant to have been haunted by an old man, although she never saw the wraith. However, writer Peggy Martyn Clark was quick to add her two-penny worth to the legend of the hotel:

> There's always some place that draws a person like a magnet. Warden Bay on the Isle of Sheppey does that to me. It has an atmosphere of long past writers; theatre folk and smugglers and ghosts. I first saw it many years ago, and time hasn't robbed it of its remoteness. Then, I was a young journalist, tired through expending too much energy through over-zealousness and wanted somewhere to relax. Lunching at a club in Chelsea I asked my friend Marian Faberge if I could stay in her bungalow on the island. She was an exotic person. Gay, bohemian, taking life as she found it and she was grand company. She agreed, of course.

At the time of Peggy's visit there was no railway to speak of and so she travelled via bus from Sheerness to Warden Point and then walked uphill. She added:

An unusual plaque on the door of one of Warden Manor's rooms..

We paused on the hilltop, looking down on an unbelievable vista of beauty. The sea stretched out along a golden strand, while a sweep of green countryside fell away sheer to the edge. The silence was broken only by the cawing of gulls. There was but a handful of artistically designed bungalows. I held my breath at the wonder of it all. That evening we walked along the beach, past some fine Tamarisk trees, to the Warden Bay Hotel, almost on the sands. It was smallish and very odd … Once inside it seemed like another world. Lit only by oil lamps, the cosiness enveloped me. Then I saw the fireplace. It took up almost the end of the room, reaching to the ceiling. It was built of stone chunks. The stones are reputed to be from old London Bridge, brought down the Thames to build the spire of Old Warden church, long since fallen into the sea. They, apparently, were gathered at low tide, brought ashore and this lovely fireplace came into being. I watched the glow from huge logs of driftwood tossed on the wide hearth. I remember one sultry summer evening listening to Freddie Bamberger playing his Concerto for the left hand. No one moved. Everything was still while the lovely notes went out over the sea. At that time he was appearing with Pam at the Chatham Hippodrome and were guests at the hotel. I have never forgotten his playing. It was at that same piano a year or so later I saw the ghost. Most of the guests had gone for the night. I sat by the fire with Madame Fab, as she was affectionately called, finishing a nightcap. We were discussing Freddie Bamberger and his playing. I was telling her how he held me spellbound. As I spoke, I turned my head towards the piano and my sentence stopped almost before it had begun. I took a deep breath then said quietly, 'there's someone at the piano.'

Marian didn't turn. 'It's the Warden ghost, I suppose,' she said airily.

I believed my writer's imagination was at work: that I was seeing things. I closed my eyes then opened them. It was still there, a faint image of a monk. In a moment of time I took in every fold of his habit, the way it hung over the stool and I watched a delicate hand move and draw it closer. Then the head turned and he smiled and was gone. I discussed it with no one. It was too vague and intangible. I didn't wish to be thought crazy. Naturally, over the years the hotel has grown apace. Modernity has crept in, yet odd enough, the end by the fireplace remains unaltered. That some strange element is there cannot be disputed. Mr Moyes who bought the place talks about the 'Funny Room'. Visitors feel a comforting presence, not knowing how to explain it, but I can still see the smiling monk sitting at that piano so long ago. Odd? Of course it's odd. Odder still when you think that Warden Bay is still as it was when I first saw it. No shops, no promenade, but one hotel by the Tamarisk trees. A hotel with a story.

The story of Warden's ghost-infested hotel doesn't end there however. In the 21 September 1962 issue of the *Sheerness Times Guardian* it was enquired if the 'Poacher's ghost' is 'still at hotel', along with a description:

The old hare-lipped poacher had a face as grotesque and uncouth as his personality. He didn't know how to love. And no one loved him. All he had in the world was an old dilapidated cottage at Warden Bay – at the time called Frog's Island – a half-starved brown terrier and an old clay pipe.

It is this grim-faced fellow who is also believed to haunt the stretch of Warden Bay, according to the paper, '… about 70 years after his death'. The cottage which belonged to this chap was at the time part of the Warden Bay Hotel, run by Fred Moyes, as mentioned previously by Peggy Martyn Clark.

According to the newspaper report, 'the old poacher's ghost has been sensed by many. And holidaymakers booking accommodation in the hotel have requested: "Anywhere – but not the 'funny room'."' Mr Moyes took over the hotel in the late 1950s with his wife Emily, but little did they realise that the ghosts of the past would still linger on the premises, and remain unwilling to move on to pastures new. However, one night the Moyes slept in what became known as the 'funny room'. It had been a particularly stormy night – as with all good ghostly tales – when they settled down in bed but Fred was soon to report that, 'After a couple of days my wife flatly refused to sleep there anymore. She said there was something uncanny about the room.'

Mr Moyes put the rumours of a ghost to one side until he was told by several customers of the ghoulish poacher. Even the hotel maid, a lady named Florrie Ford, came forward to mention the spectre and stated quite categorically that under no circumstances would she enter the haunted room. Despite his scepticism Mr Moyes decided to contact the previous hotel owners, a couple named Wright who had moved to Cranbrook. They were quite forthcoming with details of the reputed apparition and told Mr Moyes that in 1948 they had received so many complaints about the spectre that they decided to enlist the services of a psychic medium who pinpointed the area once inhabited by the poacher as a hive of paranormal activity. According to Mr Moyes the psychic went into a trance in order to attempt to contact the spirit and began to speak in gruff tones, as if the ghost had taken over her body. Apart from the spirit possession nothing else was gained from the medium and so Mr Moyes decided that the reputedly haunted room would have to be used for something else rather than a guestroom. Instead he converted it into a lounge bar, where visitors would stop by for coffee, and if they felt in the mood, they could slip a coin into the jukebox and spin one of their favourite songs.

Fred seemed of the opinion that by modernising the room it would possibly remove the spirit but, according to the article, 'People who have worked in the coffee bar, selling refreshments to holidaymakers, say they still get a shudder when they go into it.'

Stranger still, Mr and Mrs Moyes' little dog also refused to enter the coffee bar. According to the newspaper report however, no amount of activity was going to push Mr Moyes from his home. He said, 'a ghost can be a most likeable thing'.

There is one further detail to the story. Rumour has it that the miserable old poacher stashed his life savings beneath the floors of the building and that the reason that he still wanders the hotel is to make sure that his buried money remains.

Whilst on the subject of Jetty Road, in the summer of 2013 I stumbled across a website which showed lots of old postcards depicting Warden Bay as it had been in the past. I was intrigued to read a post by a person claiming to live on Jetty Road who stated that 'Although my house is only 25 years old, it was built on the site of an older one'. It seems that whoever used to live at the previous site could still haunt the area. The author of the piece, who went by the name William, added that due to leg trouble he'd spent the last few years sleeping downstairs and that on several occasions he'd heard the 'ghost' walking up and down his drive at night. He added that the unseen visitor appears to be wearing high or Cuban heels, as the footfalls are relatively loud and then followed by a sound suggesting that a bottle has been thrown in a litter bin. William, writing his account in 2012, concluded that the most recent visitation came on 22 July 2012 at 12.30 a.m. and then returned two hours later. William commented that, 'This is the first time that the ghost has come twice in one night'.

Creepy Cliffs

It's no surprise that due to its location overlooking the North Sea, Warden Bay has suffered cliff erosion over the years. The encroaching, frothing waves were certainly responsible for the disappearance of some buildings, including an old pub, over the years. Sheila M. Judge, along with numerous residents of the island, mentioned how the parish church had stood for so long on the precipice and that its old graveyard had long succumbed to the sea. However, this resulted

in, as Sheila wrote, 'tombstones, coffins and bones sticking out from the cliff face'. This would no doubt have been quite a macabre sight to anyone who braved the waters around the fragile cliff and some of these brave seamen would speak of feeling rather peculiar whilst sailing in the vicinity of waters that once quite literally swallowed a village and all of its fields. Of course, over time these cadaverous remains would eventually be swept out to sea, some of them eerily adorning the neighbouring beeches. It is said that one woman, who resided at Shellness, had collected a number of these ghastly oddments and displayed them in her house. To add to the Gothic atmosphere the woman strategically placed torches near them in order to give off a fiendish glow and cast weird shadows across the room.

There is an extremely peculiar legend from Warden concerning the mentioned church – that of St James – which succumbed to the sea many years ago. According to historian Wendy Kennett, 'I have been told of how, if you stand on the lonely cliffs at Warden Point, you can hear, on a still night, the sound of church bells ringing under the water.' St James' church was, according to Wendy,

A ghostly image of St James' church which once stood on the precipice of Warden Bay. (Image created by the author)

Cliff ahead!

'once part of the property owned by the crown until Henry III granted it to the Maison Dieu, the religious hospital of St Mary in Dover.'

Over the centuries the church had many owners and around 1636 fell into decay. Thankfully, it was restored by a county magistrate named De La Mark Banks [previously mentioned elsewhere as Delamark Banks], but by 1874 the ivy-strewn structure was literally perched on the cliff edge at Warden and eventually the concerns of one Henry Turmine – who visited the building in 1843 – were realised, as he once commented that despite its beauty, 'In all probability the land will be washed away as far as, or beyond church, in about twenty years. The sea is fast encroaching.'

In 1875 the church of St James was demolished and the remaining graves swept out to sea the following year. However, the romantic legend of this place claims that those bells still ring out – a phantom din heard by certain people on still nights. There are even those who claim that despite the church being demolished its image can be seen, emerging from the water-soaked beach. However, one only has to scour the realms of folklore to find that such a story is merely myth, and yet a popular one at that. In 2013 I published a book called *Shadows on the Sea: The Maritime Mysteries of Britain* and in it I covered a number of stories, nationwide, concerning sounds of phantom bells and alleged sightings of buildings that have long since been swallowed by the salty waves. Wendy Kennett added that, 'On a Sunday afternoon in November 1971 half a cottage, two large concrete blockhouses and a garden slid down the cliffs at Warden Point … In future years perhaps there will be a legend not only of a lost church, but of a lost village under the sea at Warden.'

At the cliff edge, looking out toward where the bells of St James' church are still said to ring out.

Warden was also said to be the home of a local witch who had curative powers, but was no doubt feared by some of the locals. There are rumours in certain quarters that the spectre of this wise woman still haunts the hamlet but despite her rather gnarled appearance, her ghost is, as in life, a rather harmless soul. Sheppey most certainly has a long tradition of folklore and suspected witchcraft (in 1651 it is recorded that a Thomas Sharpe of Minster asked jurors to give his wife – accused of witchcraft – a retrial), and it was once said that locals would hang good luck oddments and charms about their houses to ward off evil spirits. Even animals such as horses were protected by symbols of fortune to prevent them being attacked by witches. Intriguingly there were once pastures at Sheppey called Witches Field.

Such nocturnal attacks are known as being 'hag ridden' and refers to people also.

It was once believed, and greatly feared, that evil old crones would come in the night and enter people's bedrooms – as stated earlier in this book – or the stables of horses, and either straddle the animals and attempt to ride off with them, or simply exhaust them with malevolent powers. In the case of human victims, islanders were said to have been visited in the dead of night by an old hag-like spirit, which would paralyse its victim with fear and then sit across their chest, proving to be a crushing, suffocating weight. The spell would only be broken if the terrified victim could somehow snap out of the sleep paralysis by moving a finger or twitching a muscle. This bizarre, nightmarish scenario has also been called the 'old hag syndrome' and often involves witnesses who sleep on their backs. In the 1980s a Warden resident claimed to have had such an experience – waking one

The rugged cliffs around Warden are said to be haunted by smugglers.

night she realised she could not move, and sensed a horrible atmosphere in the room. Then, to her horror she saw the form of an old hag which flitted into the room, all the while mocking her with a sinister grin. The victim, unable to move, then felt the hag sit upon her chest, but after what seemed like hours of gasping for breath the woman was able to 'wake' from the astral sleep and found no sign of the invader. Such encounters are also known as 'night terrors' or a 'nightmare', which derives from the Old English 'mare', referring to a demon or goblin said to haunt the sleep of certain people by riding on their chest.

6

EERIE EASTCHURCH

The town of Eastchurch, described by historian John Marius Wilson as 'a hamlet, a parish, and a sub-district in Sheppey', is recorded in Domesday Book as Eastcryne. The town, which boasts the remains of the once glorious Shurland Hall, has been known for its smuggling history.

Haunted Water

Records from 23 October 1769 state that a Grace Davis drowned herself in the Old House pond at Eastchurch. Grace, who was married to a fellow named Isaac, was, according to researcher Augustus Daly, 'duly buried in woollen, in strict accordance with a then existing Act of Parliament'. Some folk wonder why the poor woman chose to take her own life but local gossips suggested that she had in fact been murdered by her husband. Whatever the case, Grace has never been able to rest and her ghost was said to appear on the anniversary of her death, rising from the murky depths

of the pond at midnight. Despite this being a rather forlorn tale, it seems that few have seen the ghost of the drenched woman, but what an arresting sight it would most surely be to see of a night; this unfortunate ghoul emerging from the water. Mind you, the *Gazette & Times* of 27 October 1988, probably in accordance with Halloween festivities, also reported on the well-known local spook tale:

> Local historian Mrs Lisa Tyler was working in a bar in Leysdown about twenty years ago when a couple came in, both looking deathly pale. She asked them if they were all right, and they ordered double brandies. She said, 'They told me they had been driving along when suddenly they saw a woman standing in the road in front of the car. She was wrapped in wool. They stopped the car abruptly and got out. – No one was there!!!'

Had the petrified couple seen the ghost of Grace Davis? Some say that the pond is that which can be found at the Lower Road junction facing White Horse Hill, and in the vicinity of the Post Office and the Working Men's Club, whilst author Sheila M. Judge spoke of the waterhole being situated 'adjacent to a house at the eastern end of Eastchurch High Street, where it bends very sharply right'. Whatever the case, the particular pond in question has since been filled in, but does the sopping wet ghost wrapped in wool still appear? In the *Times Guardian* of 21 August 1964 there is mention of another 'mystery woman' under the heading 'Eastchurch ghost hunt'. The article remarks that journalist and author Peggy Martyn Clark is on the hunt of 'a wrath [*sic*] of a woman' that emerges from 'a building somewhere near the Orchard at Eastchurch'. Details are vague but the report does go on to state that the mysterious figure walks towards the church before disappearing. Oddly, the snippet also states that 'there is a link maybe between this ghost and the sheep's wool thieves of over a century ago', although the article does not go into detail as to what this link is. It is interesting to note that with this vague tale, there is also mention of a ghostly woman and wool, as in the case of the spectre of Grace Davis. However, there seems to be so much confusion in so many ghostly tales, with some

A ghostly woman was said to have risen from the murky depths of the pond at Eastchurch – the place where she perished in 1769. (Illustration by Simon Wyatt)

The haunted pond at Eastchurch from an old postcard. (Author's collection)

locals confusing the haunted pond with another waterhole at Shurland Hall. And speaking of Shurland Hall …

The Sinister at Shurland Hall

According to the Eastchurch parish website, 'King Hoestan of Denmark arrived in Sheppey with 350 ships in 892 and in 893 built earthworks in the area now known as Shurland Hall.' The main structure of Shurland Hall was built in the sixteenth century, on the previous site of a thirteenth-century castle.

Sadly, all that remains of Shurland Hall is the gatehouse, but over the years the fortified manor house had many owners and distinguished visitors including Henry VIII and his soon-to-be wife Anne Boleyn who were, as guests of Sir Thomas Cheney, said to have stayed there in the October of 1532. The de Shurland family resided at

The restored façade of Shurland Hall, off the beaten track.

the manor house for more than two centuries – the descendant of Sir Jeffrey de Shurland being Sir Robert de Shurland, who was mentioned in the introduction. Some believe that, since the unfortunate passing of Sir Robert, the castle is cursed. Charles Igglesden wrote of a man who, many years ago while restoring the castle, died of an injury inflicted by a horse – or is this merely a spook story continuing the already famous legend? Either way, Sheila M. Judge confirms the suspicions, stating, 'There was reported to be a curse on anyone rash enough to live at Shurland; the tenants often died suddenly, while still young, and allegedly due to accidents involving horses.' Shurland Hall has been described as the most 'historical place in Sheppey' and such was its reputation for being a fortress that not many dared to lay siege upon it. In 2009 the BBC website reported that the hall was to be renovated but one question remained: did the reputed ghosts of the building still loiter in the area?

Charles Igglesden also wrote of a frightful spectre said to inhabit the hall. In his twenty-eighth volume of *A Saunter through Kent with Pen and Pencil* he speaks of a female informant of his who told him of many a resident spook. This woman says, 'Strangely enough I myself never had any fear, although no one else would stay in the hall at midnight in the dark. I had no fear either of the ghostly lady in black silk or the big black dog sometimes seen or of the ringing of the bells from some unknown cause.' Three ghosts in one building does seem a rather extraordinary amount, but that's not all: 'then there was the sound of the horse's hoofs outside the front door …' Of the belief that Sir Robert de Shurland still frequented the local wilds on horseback, Igglesden's informant added, '… and it was said that a hearse passed by. We would rush to the door and open it, but nothing was to be seen.' And that's not all, she continued: 'All bedroom doors were locked at night and any dog would whine if you tried to get him to pass into one of these rooms and absolutely refuse to enter. Door handles would keep turning, and fingers would run over the panels of the door.'

Considering that some villages throughout Britain are known for their handful of ghosts it seems quite amazing that Shurland Hall should boast so many within its confines, but just when you thought it was safe to turn off the bedside lamp Igglesden's source concludes that, 'Huge hairy spiders infested the place, and it was always said that they foretold death. Outside at night owls screeched and weird noises kept the inmates of the mansion awake and it was difficult to persuade guests to stay.'

I guess we can all sleep safe in our beds, however when we find that Igglesden's original article on the hall can be traced back more than a century ago. Presumably many of the spirits have long since drifted away, leaving the ominous-looking gatehouse to its own devices. Some believe it is quite possible that the woman who allegedly committed suicide in the Old House pond is the same ghostly figure seen wandering around the grounds of the hall. Around the grounds people have reported that whilst walking their dogs, their pets have refused to enter certain spots and at times freeze and cower with fear. Occasionally a peculiar atmosphere has also been felt around the murky pond. On 8 August 2013, however, a Christdeena Ellis was featured in an article for Kent Online under a heading which claimed that the 44-year-old author had 'captured [a] ghostly maid in window of Shurland Hall'. The feature was accompanied by a photo which Christdeena had taken of the hall, and appeared to show a whitish figure standing in one of the windows. The article added that Christdeena had been writing a book about the hall but

Shurland Hall was once believed to be ghost-infested.

The large pond outside Shurland Hall. People and animals have sensed a strange atmosphere in this area.

'was left scratching her head by a photo she took apparently capturing the figure of a woman in a top window'.

Mrs Ellis was always of the opinion that the hall had been ghost-infested, commenting that 'There have been major battles there and it has been built over a thirteenth-century castle so I think there is paranormal activity there definitely and I'm quite intrigued by the ghostly maid. She looks like a seventeenth- or eighteenth-century maid and she could have been a worker there.'

Sadly, the image shown by the website is extremely inconclusive and like a majority of reputed ghostly photos is open to debate; some argued that the photo could have been some type of reflection or light anomaly. Mrs Ellis added that she'd also photographed some orbs around the building, but again, these objects have

never been proven to be ghostly. Mrs Ellis sent her photograph to a paranormal investigator who commented that the image is 'very odd indeed' but many others who have looked at the photo cannot see anything untoward at all.

There is a sinister legend attached to an old tree that was said to have stood in the vicinity of Shurland Hall. Many local teenagers often told the legend to petrified friends on cold, autumnal nights as a warning not to stray too close to the haunted hall. The fable claims that if you manage to locate the correct old tree then within its twisted frame you will find a rusty knife, embedded deep within the bark. Rumour has it that the weapon was put there by a gnarled witch as part of an evil curse; should you remove the blade from the tree than you shall fall under that particular curse. Those who tell the

In the summer of 2013 a woman named Christdeena Ellis claimed to have photographed a ghost peering out of one of these windows of the hall.

story will state quite matter-of-factly that the reason the witch stabbed the tree was in the hope that it would die, along with all those who inhabited Shurland Hall. Over time this friend-of-a-friend tale has been passed through schools and colleges, including those at Minster, although it seems as if the curse remains engrained in that tree because no one has managed to remove that rusty implement – not that they can find it – probably due to fear rather than the want of trying. Such a legend, however spooky, has echoes of so many other Kent-related myths, such as the Countless Stones at Aylesford, near Blue Bell Hill where it is said that if you manage to count the correct number then you will conjure the Devil! Another similar version relates to the so-called Devil's Bush in Pluckley, near Ashford, a village thought to be Britain's

most haunted. The legend claims that should anyone be brave (or stupid) enough to visit the bush on a dark and windy night, strip off naked and dance around the scrub a certain amount of times (usually thirteen, for effect), then again, the Devil will appear. However, the 'knife in the tree legend' has closer associations with an ancient tree situated in All Saints churchyard, at Loose in Maidstone. Local teenagers will often tell you that if you stick a pin into a certain segment of the tree and take part in a certain ritual – usually by saying a certain line or rhyme of words (they vary depending on the storyteller) – then immediately after you have muttered the lyrics you must run to a certain window of the church (or a specific grave/tomb) in order to catch a quick glimpse of a spectral woman killing a baby. Hideous stuff, but complete myth!

The Shurland Hotel, which can be located on the High Street in Eastchurch, also has a history of peculiar happenings. In October 2011 Kent Online reported on the 'haunting moment' that a 'phantom glass-flinger' was caught on camera. Although paranormal activity at the hotel had been witnessed by staff and customers alike for many years, this was the first time any evidence had actually been produced to suggest that a ghost was lurking on the premises. Things took on a rather spooky turn when a pint glass full to the brim with beer was seen to fly from one of the tables and smash on the floor. The landlord, a Mr Haynes, who wasn't there at the time, was so intrigued by the incident and keen to prove it was a genuine occurrence that he immediately viewed the CCTV camera in the bar to see if it had picked up the flying pint glass. Lo and behold, the camera had picked up the extraordinary incident.

Mr Haynes told the *Sheerness Times Guardian*, 'So much stuff happens here. We've had banging on the walls and footsteps across the roof but there's nobody there.'

The landlord, who lived in the upstairs flat with his wife Sam, also spoke about the night his wife woke up and saw a little girl standing at the edge of the bed. 'The girl was about seven or eight,' he commented, but was the spirit responsible for the touch lamp in the same room flickering on and off? Mr Haynes also commented that a builder who stayed at the hotel for a few weeks had a creepy experience one morning when the bedroom door opened and a face peered in. The man jumped out of bed to investigate but there was nobody to be seen.

Mr Haynes concluded with an encounter involving a male member of bar staff, who was hit by a flying toilet roll at the top of the cellar stairs.

The footage of the alleged flying pint appeared on YouTube, but to many it remains inconclusive. There is no doubt that the glass does slide from the table but sceptics would argue that more evidence is required before suggesting a ghost is responsible. Staff at the Shurland Hotel set up a website to record any unusual happenings, but sadly it hasn't been updated for a while. Even so, the hotel is over 200 years old and was known up until the 1980s as the Crooked Billet.

The Castle pub sits close by the Shurland Hotel. In his book *Haunted Inns of Kent*, Roger Long also mentions a phantom coach and horses said to glide 'ergo between the Shurland and the Castle' although he doubts the more recent report from a man who claimed to have seen the spectral coach on the grounds that the witness was 'leaving the Shurland and heading for the Castle', suggesting that maybe the manifestation had been the product of too much alcohol!

The Shurland Hotel in the High Street at Eastchurch.

The Shurland Hotel – the haunt of a ghost that likes to move pint glasses.

The stretch of road between the Shurland Hotel and The Castle pub is believed to be haunted by a phantom coach and horses.

A Coach and Horses and More ...

A phantom carriage pulled by a spectral horse or two seems popular in folklore. One such vehicle is briefly mentioned in Peter Underwood's book *Ghosts of Kent*. He comments on Parsonage Farm at Eastchurch as being haunted over the years by '... a contraption, trotting silently by the graveyard, usually at dusk'. No one appears to know why this spectre visits the area and according to Mr Underwood, 'No one knows where it comes from or where it goes', making this spooky tale rather vague to say the least. What I've often been intrigued about regarding reputed ghostly coach and horses is the fact that we never seem to get a sighting of just the coachman floating in mid-air on his own. Surely not every coachman perished alongside his carriage, and even if he did so, surely his vehicle would not have a soul?

It's no surprise that one of Sheppey's oldest houses has a ghost story attached to it. Parsonage Farm was once owned by Cyril Poster, a former headmaster of Sheppey School. He resided at the 600-year-old house with his wife Doreen and they were said to have been accompanied by a ghost. A woman in grey supposedly loitered in the vicinity of the top landing of the house 'spiriting her way through the powder closets or disappearing in an ethereal breeze'.

Mrs Poster was far from being afraid of the lady in grey, commenting, 'She's very welcome – if she exists – and there is more than enough room for her.'

The large house has always been steeped in history and its rural setting makes it an ideal setting for tales of ghosts. According to an old *Sheerness Times and Guardian* report from the mid-1970s, 'David (12), the youngest of a talented family, has commandeered the old storeroom backing the laundry, as his "special room" – from here he has access to the top floor, by way of one of the three stair-cases and his imagination runs riot, in conversations with the "Grey Lady" before he escapes into the old priest-hole.'

According to records Parsonage Farm is believed to be a lot older than initially thought, with mention of it in *History of the Isle of Sheppey* as being in existence from AD 1130. At that time it was home to several priests.

Many old houses situated on Sheppey's sprawling marshes are said to be haunted.

7

HAUNTED HARTY

When Sheppey was often referred to as the Isles of Sheppey, Harty was very much a separate entity. Its name said to derive from the Saxon word *heord-tu*, meaning an island filled with herds of cattle. It has long been claimed that the name Harty comes from Old English and is loosely based on a term meaning 'the marsh of monsters'. Perhaps this is unsurprising when we consider other derivatives, such

The Ferry House Inn sits at the end of the 3-mile-long Harty Ferry Road. A remote location, even for a ghost!

as the name Heorot in the classic poem *Beowulf*. Heorot is the name of the great hall allegedly plagued by a man-eating monster in the ancient English poem. Historian Edward Hasted confirms my suspicions of the Saxon origination, stating that 'It is called in antient [*sic*] records Harteigh', deriving from the original *heord-tu*. The isle has also been recorded as Hertei from 1086 and in 1601 became Harty. It seems unlikely, however, that Harty was once used as the setting for the tale of *Beowulf*, with experts arguing that it more likely originated from the soggy marshes of East Anglia.

Harty is often referred to as Harty Ferry – due to the boat which used to take passengers across to the island from Oare, situated on the other side of the river. The Sheppey Website mentions how the local priest, who lived in the mainland, would use the ferry to reach the island but often due to bad weather, such as thick fog, would find himself stranded in the Swale.

Phantoms of the Ferry House Inn

A few years ago now, a paranormal investigative team visited the Ferry House Inn. This old pub sits in one of the most remote locations for any inn, on the Harty Ferry Road. Amidst the marshes, the pub is a haven for birdwatchers who can enjoy a nice drink and then look out across the landscape for unusual wildlife. The pub itself is said to date back to the sixteenth century. The warden of the ferry used to live in the house before it became a pub.

When the ghost-hunting team investigated the pub, they claimed to have taken a photograph showing the figure of a spectral man sitting at a table, accompanied by a peculiar flash of light. The researchers were of the opinion that maybe the spectre had been that of a man named Coleman who in 1854 drowned when his boat capsized in the Swale. The man was said to have lived in one of the cottages once situated where the pub now sits. The investigation, which was conducted in 2004, also revealed a strange series of banging noises in the cellar of the pub, whilst interviewed staff claimed that they'd had feelings in the past of being watched by an unseen presence. Sadly nothing substantial came to fruition.

In August of 2013 I contacted the manager of the pub, a lady named Victoria McCabe. I asked her whether any of the ghostly tales connected to the inn were true and she replied:

> There are indeed many rumours I am sure, however none of them particularly concrete. We had a psychic evening in January which picked up on a lot of spirits including those trapped here when there was a fire many centuries ago. I also understand that the owner was told by someone twelve years ago when he bought the pub never to open up the underground blocked in cellar for that sort of reason.

I guess only time will tell if anyone is brave enough to open up that sealed room but what spirits and manifestations of the night will come forth should it be opened is anyone's guess.

The thirteenth-century church of St Thomas, which can be found at Harty, is also rumoured to have a ghost. Many years ago there were sporadic sightings of shadowy figures loitering about the

The Ferry House Inn.

The thirteenth-century church of St Thomas at Harty.

grounds which led some researchers to believe that such entities were in fact ghosts of those seamen who had drowned in the Swale and were then buried in unmarked graves.

Such is the remote location of Harty I'm actually quite surprised that anyone has reported seeing such ghouls, especially when one considers that records from the nineteenth century speak of the local inhabitants as having to travel a couple of miles on pony and trap to reach the nearest town. Even so, some of the most isolated spots on this planet are also some of the most haunted, or so it would seem.

I hope you've enjoyed this trip to the Isle of Sheppey in search of its reputed spooks and spectres. I think it's only fair that I leave you with the words of Sheila M. Judge, who put so much work into highlighting the strange history of the island:

Sheppey, the wild Island, with laws and beliefs entirely its own, passes rapidly into the pages of history. The strange local tales that were once passed on down through the generations, may soon be heard no more.

Shurland Hall from an old postcard. (Author's own collection)

BIBLIOGRAPHY

Arnold, Neil, *Mystery Animals of the British Isles: Kent* (CFZ Press, 2009)

Daley, Augustus, *A History of the Isle of Sheppey* (Arthur J. Cassell, 1904)

Dolan, Mia, *Haunted Homes* (Harper Collins, 2006)

Eason, Cassandra, *Ghost Encounters: Finding Phantoms and Understanding Them* (Blandford, 1997)

Forman, John, *Islanders* (Compiled by Arts & Libraries Pub., 1996)

Harper, C.G., *The Ingoldsby Country: Literary Landmarks of the Ingoldsby Legends* (Adam & Charles Black, 1906)

Igglesden, Charles, *A Saunter through Kent with Pen and Pencil* (Kentish Express)

Judge, Sheila M., *The Isle of Sheppey* (Roadmaster Books, 1997)

Judge, Sheila M., *Strange Tales of Old Sheppey* (Tames, 2003)

Long, Roger, *Haunted Inns of Kent* (SB Publications, 2005)

Paine, Brian (ed.), *Unexplained Kent* (Breedon Books, 1997)

Rymill, John A., *The Three Sheppey Islands: In the 19th and 20th Centuries* (Green Arrow, 2006)

Underwood, Peter, *Ghosts of Kent* (Meresborough Books, 1985)

Various, *Around and About the Isle of Sheppey* (Freedom Centre Publishing, 1995)

www.clcshe.eclipse.co.uk/main.html
www.kentmonsters.blogspot.com
www.kentnews.co.uk
www.kentonline.co.uk
www.miadolan.com
www.maiwriting.com
www.minstergatehousemuseum.info
www.pbase.com
www.queenboroughguildhallmuseum.btck.co.uk
www.theroyalhotelsheerness.com
www.sheernessheritagecentre.com
www.shepherdneame.co.uk/pubs/sheerness/old-house-home
www.sheppeywebsite.co.uk
www.spitalfieldslife.com
www.theferryhouseinn.co.uk
www.theshurlandhitel.co.uk
www.voicesofleysdown.co.uk
www.youwomen.co.uk